STERLING
New York

An Imprint of Sterling Publishing Co., Inc.

ISBN 978-1-4549-4279-5 (print format)
ISBN 978-1-4549-4280-1 (e-book)

Distributed in Canada by Sterling Publishing Co., Inc.
c/o Canadian Manda Group, 664 Annette Street
Toronto, Ontario, Canada M6S 2C8
Distributed in the United Kingdom by GMC Distribution Services
Castle Place, 166 High Street, Lewes, East Sussex, England BN7 1XU
Distributed in Australia by NewSouth Books
University of New South Wales, Sydney, NSW 2052, Australia

For information about custom editions, special sales,
and premium and corporate purchases, please
contact Sterling Special Sales at 800-805-5489
or specialsales@sterlingpublishing.com.

Manufactured in Canada

2 4 6 8 10 9 7 5 3 1

www.sterlingpublishing.com

Interior design by Christine Heun
Cover design by Elizabeth Mihaltse Lindy

Picture credits—see page 261

BEDSIDE BOOK
- OF -
PHILOSOPHY

**FROM THE BIRTH OF
WESTERN PHILOSOPHY
TO *THE GOOD PLACE***

- 125 -

Historic Events and Big
Ideas to Push the Limits
of Your Knowledge

GREGORY BASSHAM

STERLING
New York

Contents

Introduction

PHILOSOPHY HAS A LONG AND EXCITING HISTORY. In some ways, however, it is an unusual history. In fields such as science, mathematics, medicine, and engineering, the major milestones can generally be viewed as unequivocal advances: stones are added to an ever-more-impressive edifice of knowledge. In philosophy, the milestones are more like insightful and thought-provoking comments in a Great Conversation. In this Conversation, one finds many fascinating insights and much food for thought, but not much—it must be admitted—in the way of indisputable knowledge or agreement. To some, like controversial American editor and satirist H. L. Mencken (1880–1956), this is a sign of failure. "Philosophy," said Mencken, "consists largely of one philosopher arguing that all the others are jackasses. He usually proves it, and I should add that he also usually proves that he is one himself." There is some truth in this remark, for philosophy is, in large part, a story of vaulting ambitions and humbled reckonings. Philosophers have sought answers; what they have found are mostly questions. This in itself is highly instructive. As Socrates (c. 469–399 BCE) vividly reminds us, a conversation that ends inconclusively can still be very much worth having. In philosophy, success is not measured in terms of clear-cut "advances" that can be added to a growing body of knowledge. Its successes lie largely in the questions themselves, and in the rich and vibrant conversations those questions can provoke as they become increasingly sophisticated and complex.

In brief, there is a special relationship between philosophy and its milestones. In philosophy, the milestones are not like buoys in a receding wake, never again to be seen as philosophers bravely sail on into uncharted new waters. Rather, the milestones are significant contributions to an on-going conversation. In that discussion, great thinkers like Plato (c. 428–c. 348 BCE), Aristotle (384–322 BCE), Immanuel Kant (1724–1804), and David Hume (1711–76) are not simply mute figures in a philosophical mausoleum; they are living voices in a fascinating dialogue that extends far into the past and will continue, one hopes, well into the future.

The Nature and Scope of Philosophy

What is philosophy? What are its proper tasks? These are themselves philosophical questions, open to debate. In early Greek philosophy, there was no clear distinction between philosophy and science. Philosophy was simply "the love of wisdom," and it encompassed any field in which significant insights into the human condition and our world were believed to be found. Over time, the scope of philosophy progressively narrowed, culminating in the ultraminimalist view of some twentieth-century linguistic philosophers that philosophers are glorified lexicographers and concept analyzers, with no role to play other than as parsers and elucidators of language. Most contemporary philosophers adopt a view somewhere in the middle between these very broad and very narrow conceptions of the proper scope of philosophy.

Though philosophers often deal with issues that may seem quite technical and hairsplitting, at its core philosophy still deals with the big questions of life that exceed the ken of the physical and social sciences: Why am I here? Does life have meaning? Does God exist? Is there life after death? Can I know what true reality is? How should I live? What should my goals and values be? What is a good society? Philosophy remains most electric and vital when it keeps in close contact with these big existential questions.

The Value of Philosophy

If philosophy is not, as I have suggested, a path to definite knowledge and assured ultimate truth, wherein lies its value? Its chief benefit lies in the way it disciplines, enlarges, and humbles the human mind.

Philosophy disciplines the mind by introducing it to a regimen and a thought world in which standards of reasoning, argumentative rigor, clarity of expression, critical scrutiny, and logical coherence are much higher than they are in ordinary life. By means of this regimen, our powers of thinking, reasoning, and effective expression are greatly augmented, and we develop defenses against the nonsense and illogic that bombard us in the media, on the Internet, and in our daily lives.

Philosophy also enlarges the mind by expanding our intellectual horizons and exposing us to visions of reality and of the good life that we may never have thought without it. In philosophy we encounter (to adapt nineteenth-century British poet Matthew Arnold's phrase) "the best that has been thought and said" about questions of meaning, value, and the urgent existential questions of life. As we grapple with life's mysteries, reading the great thinkers of the past can be of immense value. As American philosopher Tom Morris (b. 1952) has noted, these thinkers are like "native guides" who have thoroughly and skillfully explored territories that are all new to us. In studying the great philosophers, we can also achieve a better understanding of the important ideas and intellectual traditions that have shaped our world today.

Finally, philosophy humbles the mind by bringing home the depth, intricacy, and difficulty of the great questions. In many ways, the story of philosophy is a narrative of humbled ambitions. Time and again, great thinkers have claimed to discover ultimate truth, only to be shot down in flames. The lesson to be drawn from this is not that philosophy is a waste of time (Mencken's view), but that philosophy is tough sledding and rarely can produce definitive answers beyond dispute. Realizing this is itself an important kind of wisdom.

About This Book

Except for one new entry (the last), this book is a shortened version of my earlier work, *The Philosophy Book: From the Vedas to the New Atheists, 250 Milestones in the History of Philosophy* (Sterling Publishing, 2016). The "milestones" in this volume are significant ideas, events, and works in the history of philosophy. I have arranged these in chronological order, providing precise dates whenever possible, and approximate dates when exact dating is impossible. The book makes no pretense to completeness and is by no stretch an entire "history of philosophy," concise or otherwise. It is simply my personal, succinct tour of what I believe are some intriguing highlights in the story of philosophy. As bedside companions go, it may not be as stimulating (or as soporific) as some; but on that, mum must be the word.

BIRTH OF WESTERN PHILOSOPHY

Thales (c. 625–c. 545 BCE), Anaximander (c. 610–c. 546 BCE), Anaximenes (fl. c. 545 BCE)

SOCRATES SAID THAT "philosophy begins in wonder." In Western civilization, philosophy began when a group of Greek sages in the Aegean seaport of Miletus sought to satisfy their sense of wonder by asking new kinds of questions. Instead of relying on mythology and supernatural forces to explain nature, these thinkers began to use reason and observation. This marked the beginning of science as well as philosophy.

Thales has traditionally been regarded as the first Western philosopher. He was one of the Seven Wise Men of Greece and was reputed to have studied in Egypt, where he learned geometry. Some early sources claimed he successfully predicted eclipses. One anecdote relates how Thales was mocked by a servant girl for falling into a well while stargazing; perhaps to demonstrate that he was no absentminded professor, it is also said he was the first to show that there are 365 days in a year.

Thales asked whether there is some basic "stuff" out of which everything is made, and concluded that there is. Everything is made of water, he claimed. Why he believed this is unclear. Perhaps he was impressed by the fact that water can be a solid, a liquid, or a gas. Aristotle speculates that Thales was struck by the linkage between water and life, noting that seeds, for example, always contain moisture. Whatever the reasons, what is important is the kind of explanation Thales was looking for. Here, for the first time in recorded history, someone was trying to explain the natural world entirely in terms of natural phenomena.

Thales inspired others to seek similar explanations. His follower, Anaximander, suggested that the fundamental stuff is not water, but an indeterminate substance he called the *apeiron*, Greek for "boundless" or "indefinite." Not long after Anaximander, another philosopher from Miletus named Anaximenes—apparently impressed by the fact that air can become more or less dense—speculated that everything is some form of air. From such seemingly unpromising beginnings, the Western philosophical quest began.

A Dutch engraving from c. 1616 of Thales of Miletus, considered by many to be the first Western philosopher.

SEE ALSO Atoms and the Void (c. 420 BCE)

THE DAO

Laozi (fl. c. 550 BCE)

CHINESE CIVILIZATION HAS BEEN SHAPED by three major traditions: Confucianism, Buddhism, and Daoism. The oldest of these may be Daoism, but it is difficult to say because the origins of Daoism are shrouded in mystery and legend.

According to Chinese tradition, Daoism was founded by the sage Laozi around 550 BCE. Laozi is the reputed author of the classic Daoist text the *Dao De Jing* (*Classic of the Way and Power*), a short book full of memorable aphorisms and profound sayings, but not easy to understand. There is a point to this ambiguity, however, for Daoists believe that life itself is inherently mysterious. Ultimate Reality, they claim, cannot be grasped by words or concepts; it can only be felt in the pulse in moments of tranquility.

> The Dao means . . . the way of ultimate Reality, the way of the universe, and the way that humans should order their lives.

The central concept of Daoism is that of the Dao ("the Way"). The Dao means, at once, the way of ultimate Reality, the way of the universe, and the way that humans should order their lives. It is the ineffable and transcendent ground of all existence, yet it is also immanent; it orders and flows through all things. To live well is to live in harmony with the Dao, and this means to live simply, naturally, and contentedly in a way attuned to the rhythms and harmonies of nature.

In many ways, Daoism is the direct opposite of Confucianism, which is the most influential tradition of Chinese wisdom. The strong emphasis Confucianists place on book learning, active government, and elaborate ritual are all rejected by Daoists. They favor a natural, spontaneous approach to life. This idea is captured in the Daoist concept of *wu wei*, or "effortless doing." Wu wei literally means "inaction" or "nondoing," but it is not a recipe for do-nothing passivity. Rather, it is a counsel for letting things happen naturally and without meddlesome interference or unnecessary conflict. Daoists believe that people often mess things up when they try to "fix things" by passing too many laws or by trying to micromanage people's lives. In most cases, they claim, more can be accomplished by means of a less activist, more yielding approach. .

SEE ALSO Confucian Ethics (c. 500 BCE), Cynicism (c. 400 BCE)

REINCARNATION

Pythagoras (c. 570–c. 490 BCE)

WE HAVE LITTLE DEFINITE INFORMATION about Pythagoras. He left no writings, and many legends sprang up about him after his death. It is certain, however, that he had a huge impact on Western civilization. What we do know is that Pythagoras was born in Samos, a small island off the coast

of what is now Turkey, very close to Miletus. In midlife he moved to Croton, a major Greek colony on the coast of southern Italy. There he established a quasi-monastic community, open to women and men, which was dedicated to both religious and intellectual pursuits. One of the few surviving quotations attributed to Pythagoras is that "friends have all things in common."

So far as we can tell, Pythagoras was one of the first Western thinkers to believe in metempsychosis, or reincarnation. Though the evidence is uncertain, he seems to have held that the body is the soul's "tomb," that the soul is weighed down and polluted by the impurities of the body, and that the soul is fated to be reborn again and again into human and animal bodies until it finally shakes itself free from the wheel of rebirth by living a pure and religious life.

Pythagoras is famous, of course, for proving the Pythagorean theorem in geometry. Like Plato, he believed that mathematics elevates the mind and helps it to focus on what is eternal and divine. He also taught that mathematics is crucial for understanding the physical world, for nature is an organized harmony that (as Galileo would later say) is written in the language of mathematics. It was claimed that he also coined the term philosophy ("love of wisdom") to designate the rigorous intellectual work that was necessary to purify the soul and raise it to the level of divinity.

Pythagoras is also important because of his influence on Plato. Plato's beliefs in a separation of mind and body, in reincarnation, in the immortality of the soul, in the corrupting influences of the body, and in the role of philosophy and mathematics in living the best kind of human life and achieving spiritual fruition are all strongly Pythagorean. Plato is unquestionably one of the most important thinkers in Western civilization, and therefore, indirectly, so too is Pythagoras.

OPPOSITE: Pythagoras, likely the earliest Western thinker to believe in reincarnation and, legendarily, one of the earliest proponents of the round-earth theory, is shown here in an engraving by Domenico Cunego after Raphael, 1782.

SEE ALSO Ahimsa (c. 540 BCE), No-Self (*Anatta*) (c. 525 BCE), Mind-Body Dualism (c. 380 BCE)

c. 5 4 0 BCE

AHIMSA

Nataputta Vardhamana (Mahavira) (c. 599–c. 527 BCE)

THE SIXTH CENTURY BCE WAS AN EXCITING TIME to live in India. The Hindu Upanishads were being written around this period, and two major religions emerged as reactions to the orthodox schools of Hinduism. One was Buddhism; the other was Jainism, which was founded by Nataputta Vardhamana, known as Mahavira ("Great Hero" in Sanskrit), sometime in the middle of the sixth century BCE, though some scholars think it was a few decades later.

According to Jain sources, Mahavira was born in 599 BCE in northeastern India, not far from present-day Nepal. Following a privileged upbringing as part of a royal family, Mahavira decided at the age of thirty to renounce the world and seek enlightenment. Few have ever done so with greater determination. For over twelve years he wandered naked all over India, practicing extreme bodily austerities and carefully avoiding all harm to other creatures. Finally, in his early forties, he achieved complete enlightenment and release (*moksha*). For the next thirty years he taught others the path to liberation that he had discovered. He ended his own life, at age seventy-two, by voluntary self-starvation.

Like Hindus and Buddhists, Jains believe in karma and reincarnation. The ultimate goal of life, they hold, is to liberate the soul from karma and rebirth. The way they seek to do this is by practicing asceticism (self-denial, nonattachment) and trying to avoid all injury to other life forms. Jain monks pursue this path in a particularly rigorous way, taking five vows that include celibacy, complete nonpossessiveness, noninjury or nonviolence (*ahimsa*), truthfulness, and refusing to take anything that isn't given to them. Lay Jains are allowed to marry and pursue a more moderate (but still extremely disciplined) lifestyle of renunciation.

Jains believe that all living things have souls, and they take great care to avoid any unnecessary killing or harm. Mahavira himself reportedly used a broom to gently sweep the ground in front of his feet, lest he should tread on any tiny creatures. This idea of ahimsa greatly influenced many Indian schools of philosophy.

A miniature painting depicting Mahavira, founder of the Jain religion, from a c. 1503 manuscript of the *Kalpa Sutra*, a sacred Jain text.

SEE ALSO Reincarnation (c. 540 BCE)

THE FOUR NOBLE TRUTHS

Siddhartha Gautama (Buddha) (born c. 6th–4th century BCE)

This monumental bronze statue, the Great Buddha of Kamakura, in Kamakura, Japan, is shown here in a nineteenth-century photograph; the monument is believed to date to c. 1252, and stands almost 44 feet (13.5 meters) tall.

THE FOUNDATION OF BUDDHISM is veiled in clouds of myth and uncertainty. What we do know is that Buddhism was founded by Siddhartha Gautama, who lived and taught in southern Nepal and northern India sometime between the sixth and fourth century BCE. Born the son of a wealthy king, Siddhartha lived a life of luxury before becoming discontented in his late twenties and deciding to leave home to seek his enlightenment. For six years he practiced meditation and severe bodily austerities but did not find the answers he was looking for. Finally, he sat under a fig tree one day and resolved not to get up until he had achieved enlightenment. At dawn, the Great Awakening occurred and he became Buddha ("the enlightened one"). He gathered a community of disciples and spent the next forty-five years teaching the liberating path he had discovered.

What was this secret to inner peace that Buddha discovered? It is encapsulated in his "Four Noble Truths": life is suffering, the cause of suffering is selfish craving (*tanha*), suffering can be overcome, and the way to overcome suffering is by following the Eightfold Path (right views, right aspiration, right livelihood, and other beliefs and practices that signal a serious commitment to the Buddhist lifestyle and path of liberation).

Though Buddhism has become encrusted with speculative doctrine, Buddha himself always maintained a "noble silence" about metaphysical issues. One of his disciples commented, "Whether the world is eternal or not eternal, whether the world is finite or not, whether the soul is the same as the body or whether the soul is one thing and the body another . . . the Lord does not explain to me." What Buddha taught was a practical therapy for rooting out the persistent causes of unhappiness and discontent. He recognized that people live in chains forged by their own hands. We suffer because we are self-centered and thirst after empty pleasures and things we cannot have. Once we liberate ourselves from all clutching desires, we are free, Buddha said, to "cultivate love without measure toward all beings."

SEE ALSO No-Self (*Anatta*) (c. 525 BCE), Stoicism (c. 300 BCE)

NO-SELF (*ANATTA*)

Siddhartha Gautama (Buddha)(born c. 6th–4th century BCE)

IN BUDDHA'S TIME, LIKE TODAY, Hinduism was the major religion of India. Buddha agreed with some Hindu teachings, including the doctrines of karma and reincarnation, but rejected others. Among those he rejected was the Hindu idea, found in the Upanishads, of a permanent soul or self (Ātman) that is ultimately identical with the absolute Reality (Brahman). By contrast, Buddha taught that there is no soul or self in the sense of a self-identical ego, a substance that endures over time. This idea of no-self (*anatta*) is a central teaching of Buddhism, one of the three so-called "marks of existence," or dharma seals.

> Buddha believed that what people call a soul or self is really only a temporary bundle or aggregation of mental and physical features.

Buddha believed that what people call a soul or self is really only a temporary bundle or aggregation of mental and physical features (*skandhas*). These include body, perception, feelings, consciousness, and instincts or predispositions (some of which are subconscious). These five constantly changing features more or less hang together as an integrated unit while we are alive, but they do not constitute a "thing" or an "entity," and at death they dissolve or disperse. There is no soul, or "me," that survives death. This raises an obvious problem for Buddha's belief in karma and reincarnation. For if there is no enduring soul or self, what is it that gets reincarnated into another form and is the bearer of karma? Buddha's answer was that a kind of karma-laden psychic structure carries over into the next life, yet this is not a soul or self but simply an information-bearing packet of habits, predispositions, and so forth that survives death and forms the basis for a person's next incarnation.

Buddha's denial of a permanent self is related to another key teaching of Buddhism: impermanence (*anicca*). Buddha taught that reality is an ever-changing phantasmagoria, a flux in which nothing is permanent. Everything is constantly changing, so that nothing remains literally "itself" or "the same" from one moment to the next. This is part of why Buddha denied the existence of a permanent self. As he saw it, change is such a fundamental feature of empirical reality that each of us is literally a different person each second of our lives.

SEE ALSO Ahimsa (c. 540 BCE), Reincarnation (c. 540 BCE), The Four Noble Truths (c. 525 BCE)

CONFUCIAN ETHICS

Kong Qiu (Confucius) (551–479 BCE)

WITHOUT QUESTION, CONFUCIUS is one of the most influential philosophers in human history. For more than two millennia, he has molded the Chinese mind and way of life.

"Confucius" is a latinized form of Kong Fuzi ("Master Kong"); his real name was Kong Qiu. He was born in the mid-sixth century BCE near present-day Qufu, in southcentral China, and grew up poor following the early death of his father. After holding a series of menial jobs, he opened a school and became a teacher during what was a turbulent period in Chinese history, filled with constant warfare and social disorder. Throughout his long career as a teacher and public servant, Confucius sought to restore peace, good governance, and a strong social fabric to China. He believed that the key to any healthy society lies in building strong families, educated leaders, and ethical individuals. Most of his teaching focused on these themes.

Confucius looked back to an earlier period of Chinese history, the era of the so-called Sage-Kings, that he believed provided a model of a good society. This was a period when rulers led by example and displayed *ren* (benevolence, love) toward their subjects. It was also a time when people displayed both *li* (proper manners and ceremonial behavior) and *xiao* (respect for one's parents, elders, and ancestors). The stress Confucius laid on proper ritual and ceremony may be puzzling to Westerners. Why have elaborate rules about how many times one should bow, how tea should be served, how long one should mourn the death of a parent, and so forth? Confucius believed that such rules help to order our minds, calm our passions, and show proper respect to one another. They are outward symbols of inner harmonies and proprieties.

Confucius's greatest contribution to Chinese culture may lie in the field of education. Largely because of his influence, China and other Eastern cultures have historically placed great importance on educational achievement, learning, and respect for teachers. Many Asian nations, including China, South Korea, and Singapore, observe "Teachers' Day" as a national holiday. In Taiwan, Teachers' Day falls on September 28, Confucius's presumed birthday.

An illustration titled "Confucius Teaches His Principal Doctrines" from *Sketches of Confucius*, 1920, a biographical book with prints, translated by T. L. Kan.

SEE ALSO The Dao (c. 550 BCE), Reciprocity (c. 500 BCE), Universal Love (c. 420 BCE)

RECIPROCITY

Kong Qiu (Confucius) (551–479 BCE)

CONFUCIUS WAS A HUMANIST in the sense that he focused mainly on practical human concerns and said very little about spiritual matters or the ultimate nature of reality. The core of his teaching deals with questions of ethics and politics. With respect to ethics, Confucius was a thinker far ahead of his time. One example of this is his doctrine of reciprocity (*shu*).

It is said that one day Confucius's disciple Tse-kung asked, "Is there one single word that can serve as a principle of conduct for life?" Confucius replied, "Perhaps the word 'reciprocity' will do. Do not do unto others what you do not want others to do unto you." This is one of the earliest formulations of what is now called the Golden Rule. Most religions have some form or another of the rule. Jesus offers perhaps the most familiar version: "Always treat others as you would like to be treated" (Matthew 7:12). Confucius expressed essentially the same insight five centuries earlier, though he phrased the rule negatively ("Do *not* do unto others"), whereas Jesus stated it positively.

> [The Golden Rule] impels us to empathize with others, to see and feel things from their point of view.

The Golden Rule may or may not be the most fundamental rule of morality, but it certainly captures something very basic about the moral life. It rules out any kind of irrational special pleading of the form "It's

OK for me to do X, but not for anybody else to do it." It also impels us to empathize with others, to see and feel things from their point of view. This capacity for empathy is critical to human moral response.

Some critics reject the Golden Rule because they think it invites people to impose their own tastes and desires on other people. That, however, is a misunderstanding. What the rule really requires is that we try to imagine what it would be like to be in another person's shoes and then to act in accordance with that person's legitimate desires and needs. Thus understood, the Golden Rule does not compel us to satisfy desires that are, say, harmful or immoral, but only those that are reasonable and legitimate. This, of course, requires judgment, which we might get wrong. But that is true of many basic moral norms.

SEE ALSO Confucian Ethics (c. 500 BCE)

CHANGE IS CONSTANT

Heraclitus (fl. c. 500 BCE)

HERACLITUS IS THE MOST QUOTABLE of the pre-Socratic philosophers. From the 130 or so fragments of his writings that have survived, a vivid personality shines through: proud, passionate, contemptuous of the common herd, yet moved by a deep religious impulse to find unity in difference and order in apparent disorder. Like the Chinese sage Laozi, Heraclitus wrote in pithy, enigmatic aphorisms. For this reason, he was known in antiquity as Heraclitus the Obscure.

Heraclitus taught that all things are in flux. "Change alone is unchanging," he declared. Though some things appear to be permanent and unchanging, a closer look reveals that "nothing stands but for [time's] scythe to mow." "You cannot step twice into the same river; for fresh waters are ever flowing in upon you." "The sun is new every day."

Another way in which Heraclitus reminds one of Laozi is in his doctrine of the "unity of opposites." Both in nature and in human affairs, harmonies flow from the strife and tension of opposites. In the interplay of light and darkness, summer and winter, male and female, lie the creative tensions that give meaning and richness to existence. "From things that differ comes the fairest attunement."

Heraclitus offered his own take on the much-debated issue of whether there is some fundamental "stuff" out of which everything is made. His answer was fire. In ever-living fire, constantly renewing itself and transmuting all things into itself, he saw the essential pattern of the world.

The deepest source of life's goodness and harmony, Heraclitus believed, lies in what he called the "Logos" (the Greek word *logos* means "word" or "reason"), the divine word or universal reason. The Logos was not a personal god, but a fiery divine force or process ordering all things for the best through creative strife. "To God all things are beautiful and good and just; but men suppose some things to be just and others unjust."

Heraclitus's doctrine of the Logos, or universal reason, was picked up by the Stoics and contributed significantly to their teaching. It also was taken up, and given a fundamentally new interpretation, in the famous opening words of the Gospel of John: "In the beginning was the Word [Logos], and the Word was with God, and the Word was God."

> Heraclitus taught that all things are in flux. "Change alone is unchanging," he declared.

SEE ALSO The Dao (c. 550 BCE), Stoicism (c. 300 BCE), Epictetian Stoicism (c. 125)

PROTAGORAS AND RELATIVISM

Protagoras (c. 490–c. 420 BCE)

In this eighteenth-century engraving, Protagoras (standing), the first and greatest of the Sophists, lectures the younger philosopher Democritus, kneeling at left.

PROTAGORAS WAS THE FIRST and greatest of the ancient Greek Sophists, a group of wandering teachers—or what we today might call life coaches—who traveled from city to city, offering to teach the art of personal success for a handsome fee. Protagoras practiced this profession for forty years and became rich and famous in the process.

In that period of Greek history, the path to power and success was effective public speaking. Protagoras was a master at giving speeches, and he claimed to be able to teach anyone "how to make the weaker argument the stronger." He had shocking ideas about many things, including religion. According to one source, Athens expelled him for writing a book in which he declared: "As to the gods, I have no means of knowing either that they exist or that they do not exist."

Protagoras was apparently the first Western philosopher to teach a radical form of relativism. He famously pronounced that "man is the measure of all things." What he meant by this is not completely clear, but most scholars believe he embraced an extreme form of subjectivism that rejects any notion of objective truth and instead leaves truth entirely up to the individual. Whatever seems true to a particular person *is* true for that person, and there are no belief-independent "facts" that could prove such a person wrong. As Protagoras's critics quickly pointed out, this implies that all beliefs are true, including the belief that all beliefs are *not* true. Protagoras stuck by his guns, but also asserted that even though all beliefs are true, it does not follow that they are equally useful. In particular, he taught that there will always be a need for skilled teachers such as himself to teach the quickest and most advantageous ways to achieve worldly success.

Protagoras's radical relativism was seen as a threat to morals, religion, and civilization itself by many of his contemporaries. Great thinkers like Plato and Aristotle attempted to refute him by developing sophisticated theories of knowing and truth. Ultimately, Protagoras's most important legacy may be the great conversation he sparked.

SEE ALSO The Sophists (c. 450 BCE), Truth Is Subjectivity (1846)

THE SOPHISTS

THE SOPHISTS WERE A GROUP of wandering teachers who professed to teach how to achieve power and success in life, particularly through the art of public speaking. Protagoras was the first and greatest of them, but there were other well-known Sophists, including Gorgias of Leontini (c. 483–c. 376 BCE), Hippias of Elis (c. 485–c. 415 BCE), Prodicus of Ceos (c. 465–c. 395 BCE), and Thrasymachus of Chalcedon (c. 459–c. 400 BCE).

The Sophists were deeply polarizing figures in their day. Many were clearly brilliant men. Some made important contributions to grammar, rhetoric, dialectic, and other fields. Unquestionably they filled an important need, teaching people how to make an effective speech when speechmaking was the path to public success in democratic societies such as Athens. Perhaps most importantly, they contributed to the intellectual ferment of the golden age of Athens by challenging conventional ideas and fueling their era's passion for close reasoning.

At the same time, many Greeks regarded the Sophists as money-grubbing charlatans and threats to traditional morality and religion. Some, like Protagoras, taught a thoroughgoing relativism that rejected any form of objective truth or absolute values. Others, like Thrasymachus, taught that "might makes right" and that ethics is for saps. Prodicus argued that the gods were personifications of the sun, moon, and other natural objects, and was widely considered to be an atheist. Many Greeks were offended by the hair-splitting "sophisms" that Sophists sometimes offered to demonstrate their skill in reasoning. Gorgias published a book, now lost, in which he claimed to prove that nothing exists; that if anything exists it cannot be known; that if anything were known it could not be communicated from one person to another.

Socrates, Plato, and Aristotle were all deeply opposed to the Sophists and portrayed them in highly unflattering terms. Plato is by far our most important source of information about the Sophists, and he saw them as mortal threats to the ideals of objective knowledge, truth, and the values he held dear. Were his fears exaggerated? Was his portrayal of the Sophists overly negative? These continue to be issues of lively scholarly debate today.

The Sophists touted the art of public speaking, or rhetoric. Here, rhetoric is personified in an engraving by French artist Etienne Delaune, c. 1540–83.

SEE ALSO Protagoras and Relativism (c. 450 BCE), The Trial and Death of Socrates (399 BCE)

LADDER OF LOVE

Diotima of Mantinea (fl. c. 450 BCE)

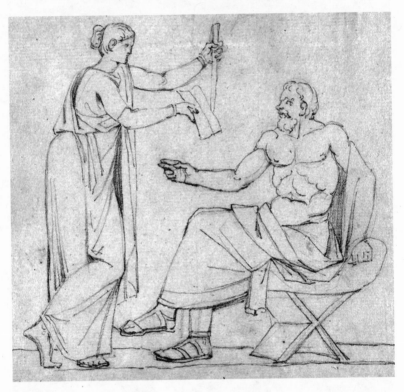

A graphite drawing of Socrates and Diotima of Mantinea by French master Jacques-Louis David, c. 1775–80; Diotima tells Socrates that there are lesser and greater mysteries of love and that we must cast our gaze to "the vast sea of beauty."

IN PLATO'S DIALOGUE the *Symposium*, Socrates says he was taught "the philosophy of Love" by a woman, Diotima of Mantinea. Scholars debate whether Diotima really existed, but she might have. Although women generally had very low status in ancient Greece, many Greek philosophers were more broad-minded. Women and men were treated as equals in the schools of Pythagoras, Epicurus, and Aristippus, and Plato shocked his contemporaries by proposing that women should receive the same education and opportunities as men. Whether real or fictional, Diotima is credited with teaching one of the most sublime views of love in Western thought.

Diotima tells Socrates that there are lesser and greater mysteries of love. The lesser mysteries are that love is a desire for beauty and for the permanent possession of the good. Love is a divinely implanted impulse that subconsciously impels people to pursue immortality through having children, creating enduring works of art, and making lasting contributions to society.

The greater mystery is that love is a ladder. We begin by loving a single beautiful individual and conceiving fair thoughts about that person. Next we observe that attractive bodies are everywhere and that all physical beauty is the same, and so we become lovers of all beautiful bodies. As we mature, we come to see that beauty of soul is more worthy of love than beauty of body. Casting our gaze still wider, we perceive that good laws and institutions have a higher kind of loveliness than any form of personal beauty. But love of laws and institutions is still love of particular things. We must cast our gaze still wider to "the vast sea of beauty," so that we perceive the high beauty inherent in all knowledge and science, being inspired thereby to "create many fair and noble thoughts and notions in the boundless love of wisdom." Fortified by these thoughts, we catch a glimpse at last of beauty itself—perfect, eternal, and changeless; the source of all lesser beauties; and the ultimate object of all forms of love and desire. Love for beauty itself, Socrates says, is the highest and truest form of love; and those who strive for the noblest things in life "will not easily find a helper better than love."

SEE ALSO Universal Love (c. 420 BCE), Know Thyself (c. 430 BCE)

KNOW THYSELF

Socrates (c. 469–399 BCE)

SOCRATES IS AN ICONIC FIGURE in Western civilization. It is remarkable what an impact this scruffy sidewalk philosopher had, both in his own time and through the centuries.

Socrates was born in Athens around 470 or 469 BCE. His father, Sophroniscus, was a stonemason or sculptor, and apparently was fairly well-to-do. As a young man, Socrates became convinced that the gods had commanded him to become a kind of philosophical missionary to his fellow Athenians. Except for periods in his forties when he served as a soldier in the Athenian army during the Peloponnesian War with Sparta, he spent his entire adult life in the streets of Athens, buttonholing anyone who would talk with him, exposing their shoddy and often inconsistent thinking, and encouraging them to join him on a quest for true wisdom and goodness. Since few people like to be shown up in public, Socrates naturally made plenty of enemies. In 399 BCE, a few years after democracy was restored in Athens following a brutal dictatorship, Socrates was put on trial for corrupting the youth and introducing strange gods into the city. He was convicted by a jury of five hundred fellow citizens and sentenced to die by drinking poison (hemlock). In prison, he spent his last days gaily discussing philosophy with his friends, refused an offer to escape, and met his death calmly and cheerfully.

One of Socrates's most constant watchwords was to "know thyself." As he went about talking philosophy on the streets of Athens, he became convinced that most people are overconfident in their beliefs. They think they know much more than they do. By being honest with ourselves and leading what Socrates called "an examined life," we can come to recognize our true condition: ignorance. Most people, Socrates taught, are in the grip of not only false beliefs but false values as well. We chase things like wealth, fame, status, and pleasure, when what really matters is wisdom and virtue. Only those who make a sincere effort to know themselves can recognize their true condition and be motivated to seek the wisdom they lack.

Socrates teaches philosophy on a street in Athens in this engraving by German etcher Daniel Chodowiecki, 1776.

SEE ALSO Ladder of Love (c. 450 BCE), The Trial and Death of Socrates (399 BCE), Socratic Dialogues (c. 399 BCE)

ATOMS AND THE VOID

Leucippus (fl. c. 440 BCE),
Democritus (c. 460–c. 370 BCE)

THE MOST INFLUENTIAL PHILOSOPHY of nature developed by the early Greek philosophers was atomism. The theory was first put forward by Leucippus, believed to be a native of Miletus, of whom we know very little. It was his student, Democritus of Abdera, Thrace, who really developed the theory.

Democritus was a prolific author, writing more than sixty books. (Unfortunately, none survive.) Among these were works on ethics, making him one of the first Western philosophers to think systematically about moral issues. Democritus believed that contentment was the goal of life. To achieve lasting happiness and freedom from disturbance (*ataraxia*), we should live a life of moderation and balance, cultivate our minds, and free ourselves from fear and superstition. Because of the stress he laid on "good cheer," Democritus was known to the ancients as "the laughing philosopher."

> [Democritus] taught that nothing exists except atoms and empty, limitless space, or void. . . . All life and thought are purely material phenomena.

Democritus also taught that nothing exists except atoms and empty, limitless space, or void. Atoms (from the Greek *atomos*, or "uncuttable") were seen as tiny indestructible particles that come in an endless variety of shapes. Atoms are eternal and exist in infinite numbers. For all eternity, atoms have swirled in ceaseless motion, combining with other atoms of similar size and shape, and innumerable worlds were created and destroyed before the current one arose. There is no purpose or design in nature; the universe is a blind, deterministic process in which necessity rules over all. Humans and other animals originally arose from primeval mud and water. Humans have souls, made up of especially fine atoms, but there is no life after death; all life and thought are purely material phenomena.

The atomism of Leucippus and Democritus might have fizzled out like most other pre-Socratic philosophies of nature except that it was embraced not long after Democritus's death by Epicurus, who did much to popularize the theory. In the first century BCE, it got another boost in the classic long poem *On the Nature of Things* by the Roman philosopher Lucretius.

As the historian Will Durant remarked in summing up Democritus's achievement, Democritus "formulated for science its most famous hypothesis, and gave to philosophy a system which, denounced by every other, has survived them all, and reappears in every generation."

SEE ALSO Epicureanism (c. 300 BCE)

UNIVERSAL LOVE

Mozi (Mo-tzu) (fl. c. 420 BCE)

MOZI ("MASTER MO") WAS AN IMPORTANT CRITIC of Confucianism who lived sometime around the end of the fifth century BCE. Very little is known about him. Since he was always defending the poor and criticizing

the wealthy, he may have come from a lower-class family. According to one account, he studied with Confucianists but came to reject many of their characteristic teachings. Instead, he founded his own school, the Mohist school, and gathered around him a loyal band of pupils who were highly skilled at fighting and formed a kind of Robin Hood force that protected the weak from the strong.

Mozi believed in a utilitarian approach to values. The ultimate test of an act or government policy is whether it benefits everyone. Many of the things Confucianists praised, such as elaborate and costly ceremonies, music, and in-depth study of the Chinese classics, Mozi condemned because they wasted time and money and did not benefit the common people.

Mozi is best known for his doctrine of universal love. He rejected Confucius's teachings that a peaceful and well-ordered society must be one in which social hierarchies are respected, and where our first loyalties must be to our parents, elders, rulers, and betters. Mozi believed that loyalties of this sort are a major source of conflict and often lead to indifference to the plight of the less fortunate. He taught that we should love and respect everyone equally. He wrote: "What is the way of universal love and mutual benefit? It is to regard other people's countries as one's own. Regard other people's families as one's own. Regard others as one's self."

Mozi believed that the gods practice universal love and so should we. To his mind, most of the bad things people do to each other are caused by selfishness, partiality, and lack of concern. The radical cure he proposed was akin to the type of universal, unselfish love (*agape* in Greek) preached by Jesus. Only when such love fills the world, Mozi believed, will the strong stop oppressing the weak, will the hungry be fed, and will peace reign.

OPPOSITE: Mozi is shown on this detail from a stamp issued in China in 2000, as part of a series of six commemorative stamps honoring great Chinese ancient thinkers.

SEE ALSO Confucian Ethics (c. 500 BCE), Reciprocity (c. 500 BCE), Ladder of Love (c. 450 BCE)

c. 400 BCE

CYNICISM

Antisthenes (c. 445–c. 365 BCE),
Diogenes of Sinope (c. 412–323 BCE)

SOME OF SOCRATES'S DISCIPLES admired him less for his teachings than for his example. One of these was Antisthenes, the founder of a philosophy known as Cynicism. He was a well-to-do Athenian who became one of Socrates's closest disciples. What Antisthenes admired most about Socrates was his moral independence, his disdain for money, fashion, and reputation, and the priority he placed on "improvement of the soul" over all else. After Socrates's death, Antisthenes opened a free school where he took such values and pushed them in a direction Socrates would not have approved. What Antisthenes taught is that civilization itself is bad and corrupting, that we should abandon government, marriage, and conventional morality and get back to a radically simpler and more natural way of living.

Antisthenes's pupil, Diogenes of Sinope, took his master's teaching to an extreme, prompting Plato to call him "Socrates gone mad." Diogenes lived on the street as a beggar, and relieved himself and had sex in public. Though he had no money or possessions, he claimed to be rich because he was satisfied with what he had. Seeing a child drink with his hands, Diogenes threw away his cup, saying "A child has beaten me in plainness of living."

As an old man living in a barrel in Corinth, it is said that Diogenes was approached by Alexander the Great. "Ask of me any favor you choose," said Alexander. "Stand out of the light," replied Diogenes. "If I were not Alexander," said the young prince, "I would be Diogenes."

For understandable reasons, Cynicism was never a very popular philosophy in ancient times. However, some of its key teachings were embraced by the Stoics. These included an emphasis on minimizing desires, avoiding excessive attachments, and regarding virtue as the sole good and sufficient in itself for happiness. An austere brand of Stoicism, taught by Epictetus around the first century CE, was heavily influenced by Cynicism. Today, Cynicism is enjoying a modest revival as growing numbers of people look to simplify their lives either to escape the rat race or to live in a more earth-friendly way. Few, however, take it to the countercultural extremes of Diogenes.

> What Antisthenes taught is that civilization itself is bad and corrupting, that we should . . . get back to a radically simpler and more natural way of living.

✳

CYRENAIC HEDONISM

Aristippus (c. 435–356 BCE)

SOCRATES HAD A NUMBER OF DISCIPLES who went on to become famous philosophers in their own right. Certainly the most surprising was Aristippus, who was born in Cyrene, an ancient city in North Africa known for its wealth. While attending the Olympic Games, he heard about Socrates and immediately went to Athens to become his pupil. For several years he was among Socrates's closest disciples. Sometime after Socrates's death, Aristippus returned to Cyrene to open a school of philosophy, where he taught what came to be known as "Cyrenaic hedonism."

Socrates believed that everyone innately desires to be happy, and that happiness (properly understood) is the greatest good. Aristippus latched on to this view and took it in a direction Socrates would have totally rejected. Aristippus taught that pleasure is the natural goal of life and that each person should pursue as much pleasure as possible. Later hedonists, such as Epicurus and John Stuart Mill, would agree with Aristippus that pleasure is the ultimate good; however, they believed that intellectual pleasures are often preferable to bodily ones and that short-term pleasures should often be avoided in order to maximize pleasure over the long run. Aristippus would have rejected such refinements. He believed that the keenest pleasures are physical and that it is foolish to postpone short-term pleasures for the sake of uncertain future ones.

Aristippus practiced what he preached. Charging a hefty fee for his teaching, he spent lavishly on fine food, expensive clothing, and female companionship. When one of his mistresses told him she was with child and that he was the father, he replied, "You can no more tell that it was I, than you could tell, after going through a thicket, which thorn had scratched you."

Aristippus would have approved of this bacchanalian scene. This mid-seventeenth-century engraving, featuring an inebriated, sleeping Pan, is by Franciscus van den Wyngaerde after Peter Paul Rubens.

Aristippus had a daughter, Arete, who also became a philosopher and succeeded him as head of the Cyrenaic school. Reputedly, she wrote forty books, so she may well have differed with her father about the superiority of bodily pleasures to intellectual ones.

SEE ALSO Ladder of Love (c. 450 BCE), Know Thyself (c. 430 BCE), Epicureanism (c. 300 BCE), Utilitarianism (1789)

THE *BHAGAVAD GITA*

THE *BHAGAVAD GITA* ("Song of God") is one of the most-loved works of Indian literature. This poem, written in dialogue form, is part of the great Hindu epic the *Mahabharata*. Countless people of all faiths have found in it wisdom and inspiration.

The book consists of a series of exchanges between Prince Arjuna and his charioteer, Krishna, who is the avatar, or earthly embodiment, of the god Vishnu. Arjuna is about to begin a great and just battle when he notices

Krishna (standing, right) preaches to the legendary prince Arjuna, in a contemporary illustration.

many friends, relatives, and former teachers in the opposing army. He hesitates, wondering whether even righteous victory and a great kingdom should be sought at such a price. Krishna reminds him that as a Kshatriya, a member of the warrior caste, he has a duty to be strong, brave, and responsible. Selfless performance of one's duties is the glue that keeps society stable and well ordered. It is also, Krishna tells him, a way of serving God and attaining liberation from worldly burdens.

Krishna goes on to describe three paths (*yogas*) to enlightenment and freedom. One, *jnana* yoga, is the way of knowledge, which pursues liberation through mystical understanding of absolute Reality (*Brahman*). The second, *bhakti* yoga, is the way of loving devotion to God. The third, *karma* yoga, is the way of action or selfless duty fulfillment without attachment or worries about the fruits of one's deeds. Krishna reminds Arjuna that even though performing our duties may seem trivial or pointless in the grand scheme of things, it is a way of worshiping God and working off and avoiding bad karma.

One measure of the popularity of the *Bhagavad Gita* is the large number of commentaries that have been written on it by major Indian thinkers, including Shankara, Ramanuja, Sri Aurobindo, and Sarvepalli Radhakrishnan. Gandhi said of it, "When doubts haunt me, when disappointments stare me in the face, and I see not one ray of hope on the horizon, I turn to *Bhagavad Gita* and find a verse to comfort me; and I immediately begin to smile in the midst of overwhelming sorrow. Those who meditate on the *Gita* will derive fresh joy and new meanings from it every day."

SEE ALSO Monism (c. 810)

THE TRIAL AND DEATH
OF SOCRATES

Socrates (c. 469–399 BCE),
Plato (c. 428–c. 348 BCE)

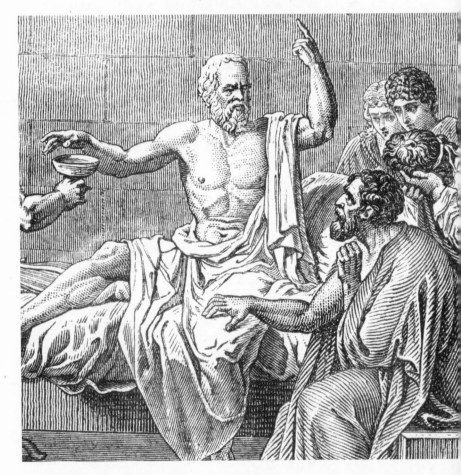

Socrates addresses his grieving disciples before drinking the cup of hemlock in an engraving from 1876.

AFTER WINNING ITS LONG WAR with Athens in 404 BCE, Sparta overthrew the Athenian democracy and imposed a puppet government of thirty pro-Spartan oligarchs known as the Thirty Tyrants. One of the leading members of the Thirty, Critias, was an associate of Socrates and a relative of Plato. Following an eight-month reign of terror, the Thirty were overthrown and the democracy was restored. As a former teacher of Critias and a well-known critic of democracy, Socrates was not popular with the new democratic leaders in Athens, and in 399 BCE he was brought to trial on charges of impiety and corrupting the young.

Plato's account of Socrates's trial in the *Apology* (c. 390 BCE) is one of the great masterpieces of Western literature and philosophy. In Plato's account, Socrates skillfully rebuts the two charges against him but in the end flat-out refuses to do what the leaders of the Athenian democracy clearly wanted him to do, namely to stop practicing philosophy. "Men of Athens," he said to the jury, "I honor and love you; but I shall obey God rather than you." As Socrates saw it, his service to the gods was a great blessing to the people of Athens, and he preferred death to abandoning his divine mission. Remarking that "no evil can happen to a good man, either in life or after death," he refused to plead with the jury or to bewail his fate. Instead, he spoke calmly about death, saying that "there is great reason to hope that death is a good." As Socrates saw it, death was like either an eternal dreamless sleep or a journey to a blessed realm in which he could converse happily with the gods and Greek heroes of old. His final words to the jury were "The hour of departure has arrived, and we go our ways—I to die, and you to live. Which is better God only knows."

Following his death, his disciple Plato memorialized him, saying "Of all the men of his time whom I have known, he was the wisest and justest and best."

SEE ALSO Know Thyself (c. 430 BCE), Socratic Dialogues (c. 399 BCE)

SOCRATIC DIALOGUES

Plato (c. 428–c. 348 BCE)

AFTER SOCRATES'S DEATH, a number of his disciples, including Aeschines, Antisthenes, and Aristippus, wrote books in dialogue form celebrating his memory. Books of this sort, which Aristotle called Socratic *logoi* (conversations), became something of a literary genre in fourth-century Greece. By far the greatest writer of Socratic *logoi* was Plato.

Plato was a wealthy Athenian aristocrat who originally planned to enter politics but decided instead to devote his life to philosophy after meeting Socrates and witnessing the political troubles of his day. After Socrates's execution, Plato traveled widely and probably began writing what are termed the "early dialogues," including such well-known works as *Apology*, *Crito*, and *Euthyphro*. The main character in those dialogues is Socrates, who emerges as an unforgettable personality: homely in body but concealing a mind and character of the finest gold. The Socrates of these early dialogues is merely a humble seeker of wisdom; he claims to know nothing except his own ignorance. By means of his famous Socratic (or "elenctic") method of question-and-answer, he punctures false claims to knowledge, pursuing a deeper understanding of moral concepts and what it means to live a good human life.

> The Socrates of these early dialogues . . . punctures false claims to knowledge, pursuing a deeper understanding of moral concepts.

Invariably, these early dialogues end inconclusively, with valuable insights gained but no final conclusions reached. The only rock-solid convictions that emerge in these conversations are the critical importance of leading an "examined life" and caring more about the "greatest improvement of the soul" than about such things as money, status, or fame.

In Plato's later writings, a quite different Socrates emerges. Instead of being an unassuming seeker of knowledge who claims to know nothing, Socrates confidently lays out grand theories of ethics, politics, knowledge, the soul, the afterlife, and the ultimate nature of Reality. This shift is part of what scholars call the "Socratic problem": the difficulty in determining what the real Socrates was like, given the limited and sometimes conflicting sources of information we possess. The general view among scholars is that in Plato's later dialogues, he is actually espousing his own developing philosophical ideas, but there is no certain way of disentangling Socrates's views from Plato's.

SEE ALSO Know Thyself (c. 430 BCE), The Trial and Death of Socrates (399 BCE)

MIND-BODY DUALISM

Plato (c. 428–c. 348 BCE)

ONE OF PLATO'S MOST IMPORTANT IDEAS involves his distinction between mind and body—what philosophers call mind-body dualism. Probably due to the influence of Pythagoreanism and an Eastern-inspired Greek religious movement known as Orphism, Plato believed that human beings are composed of two radically different parts: a physical body and a nonphysical soul. For Plato, the union of body and soul is not a happy one. The soul is immortal and existed before the body. Perhaps for some primeval sin, the soul is temporarily imprisoned in the body, where it is constantly hindered and weighed down by the body's distractions and appetites. A wise person takes little interest in food, drink, sex, or bodily pleasures; her goal is to free the soul from the corruptions of the body and focus on higher, nobler, and more lasting things. When we die, our souls leave our bodies and go off to some kind of afterlife, and many souls will later be reincarnated in another body, human or otherwise. Only those who have purified their souls through philosophy will enjoy a "blessed" afterlife. For this reason, philosophy is a preparation for death, and the true philosopher "is always pursuing death and dying."

In Plato's magnificent dialogue the *Phaedo*, he presents a number of arguments to try to prove the immortality of the soul. One is the argument from simplicity. Briefly, it goes like this: Things do not just vanish or cease to exist. The only way something can be destroyed is by breaking it apart into its component parts—for example, by smashing it with a hammer, burning it, or blowing it up. But the soul is not a physical object. It has no parts. Therefore, the soul cannot be destroyed. By its very nature, it is immortal.

Plato's dualistic view of mind and body had a profound influence on Western civilization. Largely due to Plato, belief in the immortality of a spiritual soul entered into Jewish, Christian, and Islamic thought and became a widely held view. Today, most philosophers reject dualism, though it continues to have many articulate defenders.

An engraving of a bust of Plato by Lucas Vorsterman after Peter Paul Rubens, c. 1620.

PLATO ARISTONIS F. ATHENIENSIS
Ex marmore antiquo

SEE ALSO Reincarnation (c. 540 BCE), *Meditations on First Philosophy* (1641)

PLATO'S *REPUBLIC*

Plato (c. 428–c. 348 BCE)

IN HIS MASTERWORK THE *REPUBLIC*, Plato sketches the world's first utopia, or ideal society. In Plato's day, Greece was divided into a constellation of relatively small city-states. Dictatorships, clashes between rich and poor, and civil unrest were commonplace. In Plato's view, the two major causes of bad government were self-interestedness (rulers who pursued personal gain at the expense of the common good) and incompetence (rulers who lacked the wisdom to govern well). In the *Republic*, Plato offers a radical solution to both of these root causes of poor government.

As Plato saw it, a good and well-ordered society would be a bit like a successful and well-coached sports team. Everybody would work together under effective leadership, each doing what he or she does best, to make the community as good as it can possibly be. To achieve this kind of team-oriented social cohesion, Plato proposed an elaborate system of testing and education. All citizens, both male and female, would go through a lengthy system of public education. The goals of the educational process would be threefold: (a) to create a citizen-body that is well educated and committed to the common good, (b) to determine what social role each citizen would be best at, and (c) to select "philosopher-rulers" who are both wise and public-spirited.

To ensure that only the smartest and most experienced people became rulers, Plato proposed that each prospective ruler undergo a rigorous process of testing and education lasting fifty years. This would guarantee that rulers would be wise and competent. The harder challenge, Plato believed, is to prevent rulers from abusing their power for personal gain. To achieve this, Plato's philosopher-rulers would be required to live Spartan, austere lives. They would not be permitted to possess money or to own personal property or even to have a family life. Instead, they would live in military-type barracks, eat simple meals together, and mate only with state-approved partners in order to produce the best possible offspring.

Very little of this sounds "utopian" to most contemporary readers. But Plato believed that bad government is a huge and chronic source of human misery. Only a radical fix, he was convinced, could solve such deep-seated problems.

Plato proposed that each prospective ruler undergo a rigorous process of testing and education lasting fifty years.

SEE ALSO Mind-Body Dualism (c. 380 BCE), *Utopia* (1516)

ARISTOTLE ENROLLS IN THE ACADEMY

Aristotle (384–322 BCE)

PLATO AND ARISTOTLE ARE UNQUESTIONABLY two of the greatest philosophers of all time. Although Aristotle studied with Plato for twenty years and clearly revered him, they were very different types of thinkers. Whereas Plato emphasized abstract thinking, such as math, and tended to focus on otherworldly concerns, Aristotle's thoughts were practical,

Plato (pointing skyward) and Aristotle stand at the center of a grouping of famous Greek philosophers, in this c. 1560 print by Italian engraver Giorgio Ghisi after Raphael's masterpiece *The School of Athens* (1509–11).

empirical, and scientific. The fact that two such outstanding geniuses with such different personalities were master and pupil for so many years is truly amazing.

Aristotle was born in Stagira, a Macedonian seaside town in northern Greece. His father was personal physician to the king of Macedon. Around age seventeen, Aristotle traveled south to enroll in Plato's Academy in Athens. Plato was about sixty years old at the time and immersed in the dense and highly technical speculations that are reflected in his later dialogues. Although all of Aristotle's early writings are lost, we know from various sources that as a youth his thinking was deeply imbued with Platonism. Like Plato, he wrote engaging and finely crafted dialogues. Also like Plato, he sharply distinguished soul from body, affirmed the preexistence of the soul, and offered proofs of the soul's immortality. Over time, however, Aristotle's views began to diverge from Plato's. When Plato died at the ripe age of eighty or eighty-one, Aristotle might have expected to succeed him as head of the Academy. Instead, Speusippus, Plato's nephew, was chosen. Aristotle then left Athens, traveled widely, and served as tutor to the young Alexander the Great. In 334 BCE, Aristotle returned to Athens, where he founded his own school, the Lyceum. He died at age sixty-two at the height of his career.

Despite his later differences from Plato, Aristotle was always conscious of the debt he owed to his great teacher. In Plato's Academy, Aristotle was part of a close-knit community of scholars and truth-seekers where, as Plato said in one his letters, the deepest insights arose "only out of much converse" and "a life lived together." In such a community, exciting ideas flow from mind to mind like "a light kindled from a leaping flame." Perhaps Plato was thinking of some of his talks with the young doctor's son from remote Macedonia.

SEE ALSO *Nicomachean Ethics* (c. 330 BCE)

NICOMACHEAN ETHICS

Aristotle (384–322 BCE)

EXCEPT FOR THE BIBLE, no book has influenced Western thinking about morality and the good life more than Aristotle's *Nicomachean Ethics*. Yet Aristotle's book is not what we would expect from a work with "ethics" in its title.

The book's main focus is what it means to live a flourishing and successful life. Aristotle believed that everything in nature has a *telos*, a natural end or goal. The telos of a living thing is to fulfill its nature by realizing its potentialities. The telos of a lion, for example, is to be a great specimen of lionhood, living a great leonine life. In like fashion, the natural goal and ultimate good of a human being is to be a great person living a great human life. This is what Aristotle calls *eudaimonia*, a word that is often translated as "happiness" but really means something closer to "flourishing" or even "the ideal life." But what does it mean, exactly, to "flourish" as a human being?

Two things must be considered, Aristotle says: the quality of the human being, and the quality of the life he or she is leading. To be an outstanding human being is to be a flourishing specimen of humanity, to possess excellence (*arete*) of mind, body, and character. To live an outstanding life is to live a life that is both rich in excellent activities and fortunate

> Two things must be considered, Aristotle says: the quality of the human being, and the quality of the life he or she is leading.

in what Aristotle calls "external goods" (good birth, many friends, ample wealth, good health, and so forth). An outstanding person who lives an outstanding life right up to the point of his or her death has achieved the human telos and is, in Aristotle's robust, objective sense, "happy."

At the end of the *Nicomachean Ethics*, Aristotle adds an important wrinkle to this account. He argues that the highest form of human excellence is *intellectual* excellence and, more specifically, theoretical contemplation (*theoria*). By spending as much time as possible thinking about the noblest things in the universe, we imitate the gods and their supremely blessed lives. Not surprisingly, then, Aristotle thinks that the happiest life is the life of the philosopher—a view that many of my students see as a tad overzealous.

SEE ALSO The Revival of Virtue Ethics (1981)

MAYBE LIFE IS A DREAM

Zhuang Zhou (Zhuangzi) (c. 369–286 BCE)

NEXT TO LAOZI, ZHUANGZI ("MASTER ZHUANG") is the most important figure in Chinese Daoism. We know little about him, other than what
we can infer from scattered references in a collection of writings called the
Zhuangzi. His real name was Zhuang Zhou, and reportedly he was a minor
official in the town of Meng, in central China, but he seems to have spent
most of his life as a teacher and recluse.

Zhuangzi is delightful to read because he writes in a playful, fanciful,
paradoxical, and sometimes humorous way. Often he speaks in parables that
take the form of mini-dialogues, sometimes with human participants but
frequently with animals, mythical creatures, or even personified forces of
nature such as the wind. There are recurrent themes of skepticism, relativism,
and nature-mysticism in his thought. Generally, he tried to free people from
the illusions that flow from analytical thinking and purely human-centered
perspectives. We think we possess objective knowledge and have carved up
reality into the correct categories of "this" and "that." In reality, Zhuangzi
taught, all knowing is relative and all apparent opposites are unified in what
he called the "equality of things" in the all-embracing Dao.

One of the stories he told to illustrate the limitations of human knowledge is called "Three in the Morning." A zookeeper told a group of monkeys that they would receive three acorns in the morning and four in the
evening. They were upset, so he said they could have four acorns in the
morning and three in the evening. This made them happy. The monkeys
were bent out of shape, Zuangzi says, because they thought that something
was different when it was really the same. Moral: we humans do the same.

One day Zhuangzi dreamed he was a butterfly. When he awoke, he real-
ized that he was only dreaming. But then it occurred to him that he really

did not know if he was a human who dreamed he was a butterfly or a butterfly that was now dreaming he was a human. Is it possible, he wondered, that everything we call life is part of some "great dream"?

Zhuangzi Dreaming of a Butterfly, mid-sixteenth century, an ink on silk drawing by Lu Zhi.

SEE ALSO The Dao (c. 550 BCE), Monism (c. 810)

EPICUREANISM

Epicurus (341–270 BCE)

EPICURUS WAS WHAT WE TODAY CALL A HEDONIST. Hedonists believe that pleasure is the sole intrinsic good, or that pleasure is the proper goal of life. In ancient times, there were two major schools of hedonism. One was Cyrenaic hedonism, founded by Socrates's disciple Aristippus. The other was Epicurean hedonism, founded by Epicurus. Aristippus's version was pretty crude, emphasizing instant gratification of bodily appetites. Epicurus's version was more refined, stressing pleasures of the mind over pleasures of the body and recognizing that a continuous attitude of "going for the gusto" can sometimes land one in a boatload of trouble.

Epicurus was born in Samos, on what is now the west coast of Turkey, in 341 BCE. At eighteen he came to Athens and studied philosophy with Platonists, Aristotelians, and Democritean atomists. Eventually, he opened his own school in Athens, called the Garden. Remarkably, his school was open to women as well as to men, and to people of all social classes, including slaves and prostitutes. Epicurus taught in the Garden for over thirty-five years. He was revered by his pupils and wrote some three hundred works. Unfortunately, only a few short writings survive.

With a few minor modifications, Epicurus accepted the atomism of Democritus. Everything, he believed, is made of atoms. There is no divine providence, no afterlife, and no gods that can be moved by prayer or sacrifice. All that matters, therefore, is making the most of this life. Our goal should be to live as pleasantly as possible, but this requires thoughtfulness and self-discipline. Smart people recognize that long-term pleasures outweigh short-term pleasures, and that pleasures differ in quality as well as quantity.

As Epicurus saw it, the best pleasures are those of mental tranquility (*ataraxia*), friendship, freedom from pain, and intellectual interests that excite and engage our minds. By all accounts, Epicurus led a restrained, even austere, life as far as bodily pleasures go, living a secluded existence with his friends and students, and eating and drinking sparingly. For him, philosophy was above all a form of therapy. "Vain is the word of a philosopher which does not heal any suffering of man," he wrote.

> Epicurus's version [of hedonism] was more refined, stressing pleasures of the mind over pleasures of the body.

SEE ALSO Cyrenaic Hedonism (c. 400 BCE), Atoms and the Void (c. 420 BCE), Utilitarianism (1789)

c. 300 BCE

STOICISM

Zeno of Citium (c. 334–c. 262 BCE)

ONE OF THE MOST INFLUENTIAL PHILOSOPHICAL SCHOOLS of ancient times was Stoicism. The founder of Stoicism was Zeno, who was born in Citium on the island of Cyprus and came to Athens as a young man. There, partly as a result of reading Plato's *Apology*, he decided to devote his life to philosophy. After studying with many Athenian philosophers, including the Cynic Crates, he opened his own school. Because Zeno taught from a colonnaded porch, or stoa, his school was called Stoicism.

"Nothing bad can happen to a good man," Socrates had said. Zeno took this literally and pressed it to its ultimate conclusion.

Since only fragments of Zeno's writings have survived, it is difficult to separate his teachings from those of later Stoics, although it's likely that the main tenets of Stoic doctrine go back to him. These doctrines include: that everything is made of matter; that the world is wisely and providentially governed by God (the fiery and all-pervasive divine Logos, as Heraclitus taught); that everything happens for the best and is fated to happen as it does; that all persons contain a "spark" of the divine Logos and so are all co-equal children of God and of the cosmos; and that moral goodness is sufficient for happiness, and the only thing that is categorically "good."

Zeno's most important teaching deals with the idea of inner strength and mental tranquility. What Zeno particularly admired about Socrates was the way he always stood strong and upright, no matter what life threw at him. "Nothing bad can happen to a good man," Socrates had said. Zeno took this literally and pressed it to its ultimate conclusion. If a person is truly good and virtuous, then things like death, pain, sickness, or imprisonment are not really "bad" (though Zeno does concede that they are "dispreferred"). It follows that we should approach life's hard knocks without fear, disappointment, or regret, but instead with fortitude, acceptance, and equanimity. We should stand like a rock, firm and unmoved, through all the storms of life. As English poet William E. Henley put it in his poem "Invictus" (1888):

> It matters not how strait the gate,
> How charged with punishments the scroll,
> I am the master of my fate:
> I am the captain of my soul.

SEE ALSO Change Is Constant (c. 500 BCE), Know Thyself (c. 430 BCE), Epictetian Stoicism (c. 125), The Philosopher-King (180)

INNATE GOODNESS

Mencius (Mengzi) (c. 372–c. 289 BCE)

THE TWO MOST IMPORTANT CHINESE PHILOSOPHERS are Confucius and his devoted disciple and interpreter, Mencius. Often referred to as the "Second Sage" of Confucianism, Mencius is best known for his teaching that human nature is good and his deep understanding of moral psychology.

In China, Mencius is known as Mengzi ("Master Meng"). Born as Meng Ke, Mencius was raised by a widowed mother who sacrificed greatly so that her son could receive a good education. Trained in Confucianist philosophy by followers of Confucius's grandson, Zisi, Mencius became a famous scholar by the age of forty and spent many years as a public intellectual working for political reform and defending Confucianism against hostile critics, such as the Mohists and the Daoists. After his death, Mencius's disciples published his writings and discourses in a work known simply as *Mengzi*. For centuries it has ranked with the major works of Confucius himself, among the so-called "classics of Confucianism."

In Western philosophy and religion, there has been a long-running debate between those who think that human beings are naturally good (e.g., Jean-Jacques Rousseau [1712–78] and William Wordsworth [1770–1850]) and those who think that human nature is fundamentally evil or corrupt (e.g., John Calvin [1509–64] and Thomas Hobbes [1588–1679]). A similar debate occurred in Chinese philosophy. Mencius believed strongly that people are innately good. All of us, he taught, are born with certain positive emotional predispositions, such as compassion and shame, which incline us to be good. These good emotions, if properly cultivated, can blossom into stable moral virtues, such as wisdom and propriety. According to Mencius, the two most important virtues are benevolence (*ren*) and righteousness (*yi*). Because all human beings are innately good, all are fundamentally equal and

This c. sixteenth-century ink scroll, *Educating a Son*, shows young Mencius and his mother moving to a new house; their servant (far right) carries Mencius's books. According to Mencius, anyone can preserve or recover the original, innate goodness they were born with, their "child's-heart."

all possess great potential. Given the right education and the right environment, anyone can preserve or recover their original goodness. "The great man," Mencius said, "is he who does not lose his child's-heart."

SEE ALSO Confucian Ethics (c. 500 BCE), *Emile* and Natural Education (1762)

UNIVERSAL MORAL LAW

Marcus Tullius Cicero (106–43 BCE)

CICERO IS BEST KNOWN AS AN ORATOR and Latin stylist, but he is also an important figure in philosophy. He was not an original thinker; his importance lies as a translator and transmitter of Greek philosophical ideas. One of the most significant Greek ideas he passed along is the Stoic notion of universal moral law.

Marcus Tullius Cicero was born in Arpinum, in south-central Italy, to a well-to-do family. He received a superb education, learning Greek at an early age and later studying philosophy and rhetoric in Athens and Rhodes.

> One of the most significant Greek ideas [Cicero] passed along is the Stoic notion of universal moral law.

Cicero spent most of his career in public life, as both a lawyer and a statesman. Toward the end of his life, however, he found time to write philosophy. He was an eclectic, drawing freely from Platonic, Stoic, and Aristotelian sources.

On most matters, he was a skeptic, agreeing with the Platonist Carneades that certainty is impossible and that we must make do with probable opinions. In ethics, though, Cicero agreed mostly with the Stoics. While he rejected some of the more extreme Stoic doctrines, he agreed with their ideas about divine providence, the universal fellowship of mankind, fundamental equality, and virtue as the most important object of human striving. He also concurred with their view of what they called "natural law." The Stoics distinguished human law, which changes, varies from place to place, and is often unjust, from a perfect and eternal law that emanates from the Logos (Cosmic Reason, or God).

Cicero describes this higher law in a classic passage from his *De re publica* (*On the Republic*, 51 BCE) that greatly influenced later Western thinking on law:

> True law is right reason in agreement with nature; it is of universal application, unchanging and everlasting; it summons to duty by its commands, and averts from wrongdoing by its prohibitions.... We cannot be freed from its obligations by senate or people, and we need not look outside ourselves for an expounder or interpreter of it. ... [O]ne eternal and unchangeable law will be valid for all nations and all times, and there will be one master and ruler, that is, God, over us all, for He is the author of this law, its promulgator, and its enforcing judge.

SEE ALSO Stoicism (c. 300 BCE), Epictetian Stoicism (c. 125), The Philosopher-King (180)

EPICTETIAN STOICISM

Epictetus (c. 55–135 CE)

BY A CURIOUS TWIST, the thinker who taught ancient Greeks and Romans the deepest truths about human freedom was born a slave. That man was the Stoic philosopher Epictetus.

Epictetus was born in Hierapolis, in what is today southwestern Turkey. As a slave, he was passed from one owner to another (apocryphally, one of them is said to have maimed Epictetus's leg) until he eventually wound up in Rome. There he became the property of Epaphroditus, a powerful official in the court of the Roman emperor Nero. Eventually, Epictetus was freed and rose to become a well-known philosopher in Rome. Around age forty, he was expelled from Rome by the emperor Domitian—along with other philosophers—and settled in Nicopolis, a city in western Greece. There he opened a school of Stoic philosophy and lived a simple life with few possessions.

One of Epictetus's pupils, Arrian, wrote down the master's words and published them in two books, known today as the *Discourses* and the *Manual* (or *Enchiridion*). Both books are highly readable, full of simple, powerful sayings, bluff talk, and wry humor.

Epictetus taught a stern, demanding form of Stoicism that hearkened back to the heroic days of Socrates and early Greek Stoicism. For Epictetus, philosophy was not something you "studied," but a total commitment to an arduous but deeply liberating and fulfilling way of life.

Epictetus's key idea was the importance of "acceptance." Like all Stoics, he believed that the universe was wisely governed by a kind of all-pervading cosmic reason or divine intelligence that the Stoics called Logos. Whatever happens in life must ultimately be "for the best." It follows that we should not grumble or complain when "bad" things happen in our lives, for all things eventually work for good in ways we cannot understand.

Hard knocks and adversities are inevitable in life, Epictetus taught. Most of the things people chase after—money, power, fame, a happy family life—are partly matters of luck and not fully within our control. The secret to happiness is to focus on the few things in life you *can* fully control: your own attitudes, judgments, and reactions. Make up your mind to think positive thoughts, and nothing can force you to think negative ones.

Epictetus's key idea was the importance of "acceptance." . . . Focus on the few things in life you can fully control.

SEE ALSO Stoicism (c. 300 BCE), Universal Moral Law (51 BCE), The Philosopher-King (180)

THE PHILOSOPHER-KING

Marcus Aurelius (121–180)

MARCUS AURELIUS, EMPEROR OF ROME from 161 to 180 CE, may have come closer than anyone to fulfilling Plato's dream of a philosopher who became king. Marcus was born into a wealthy, politically connected family in Rome. His father died when he was a small child, and he was brought up

Emperor and philosopher Marcus Aurelius, depicted in an
eighteenth-century engraving after an antique bust.

by his grandfather. Marcus was given a first-class education, which included a solid grounding in Greek and numerous philosophy tutors. At age eleven, under the influence of a Stoic tutor, Marcus determined to live as a philosopher, donning the coarse woolen cloak that philosophers typically wore and sleeping on the floor. At age sixteen, Marcus was adopted by the then emperor-elect, Antoninus Pius. When Antoninus died in 161, Marcus succeeded him as emperor.

Though he hated war and was always in poor health, Marcus spent much of his reign away from Rome, protecting the empire's northern borders. Once, when visiting Athens, he walked the streets in a philosopher's cloak, unguarded, attending lectures by distinguished philosophers and participating in discussions, speaking fluent Greek. When he departed, he founded chairs for each of the four major philosophical schools in Athens (Platonic, Aristotelian, Stoic, and Epicurean). At age fifty-eight, after a Roman victory over northern tribes (likely near present-day Vienna), Marcus felt death approaching. He retired to his tent, refused all food and drink for six days, and died on his own terms.

After his death, a notebook was discovered in Marcus's tent, written in Greek, titled "Thoughts to Myself," standardly translated with the title *Meditations*. In these pages, we find the authentic voice of Socrates and Epictetus, written by a man who possessed absolute power but chose instead to play the role of a dutiful servant. Here, on the banks of the Danube, Marcus meditated on the Stoic themes he'd learned in his youth: the vanity of fame, the importance of duty, the brevity of human existence, the pointlessness of fear of death, and acceptance of one's fate as part of God's wise governance of the universe. In Marcus, we find one of the very few exceptions to the maxim that "power corrupts, and absolute power corrupts absolutely."

SEE ALSO Universal Moral Law (51 BCE), Epictetian Stoicism (c. 125)

OUTLINES OF PYRRHONISM

Pyrrho of Elis (c. 360–c. 270 BCE),
Sextus Empiricus (fl. c. 200)

THERE WERE TWO MAJOR FORMS OF SKEPTICISM in ancient Greece and Rome. One was Academic Skepticism, founded around 270 BCE by Arcesilaus (c. 316–c. 241 BCE) and centered in Plato's Academy. The other was Pyrrhonian Skepticism, founded by Pyrrho of Elis.

Little is known about Pyrrho. Reputedly, he accompanied Alexander the Great on his conquest of the East. While in India, he encountered a group of "naked wise men" (yogis). Apparently they made an impression, because when Pyrrho returned to Greece he set up a school devoted to the pursuit of mental tranquility (*ataraxia*) through skeptical suspension of belief. The people of his hometown, Elis, in western Greece, were so impressed that they made him high priest, erected a statue in his honor, and exempted philosophers from taxation.

> The Pyrrhonian Skeptics held that no belief is more plausible than any other, [therefore] probability cannot be the guide of life.

By good fortune, a clear picture of Pyrrhonian Skepticism was preserved in a treatise by an obscure Greek physician, Sextus Empiricus: *Outlines of Pyrrhonism*. What emerges is an elaborate form of skepticism even more radical than the Academic Skepticism of Arcesilaus and Carneades (c. 214–c. 129 BCE).

According to Sextus's text, philosophy is both a disease and a cure. It is a disease because it leads to unhappiness and arrogant dogmatism. Philosophy promises wisdom and consoling answers, but it can provide only endless questions. The solution is to adopt a kind of meta-philosophy—namely Skepticism—that recognizes that ignorance is simply the human condition and that is content with this inescapable reality. The core of skepticism, Sextus taught, lies in the ability to construct equally forceful arguments for or against any thesis. A wide variety of argumentative strategies, called *modes* or *tropes*, is laid out to assist in this balancing process. Unlike the Academic Skeptics, who generally recognized that some beliefs are more probable than others, the Pyrrhonian Skeptics held that no belief is more plausible than any other. For this reason, probability cannot be the guide of life. Instead, we should follow our natural feelings and the laws and customs of our community.

Pyrrhonian Skepticism seems to have pretty much died out in the ancient world not long after Sextus's lifetime. In the sixteenth century, however, Sextus's writings were rediscovered, sparking a renewed interest in ancient Greek Skepticism.

SEE ALSO The Ontological Argument (1078)

NEOPLATONISM

Plotinus (c. 205–270)

PLOTINUS IS THE GREATEST GREEK PHILOSOPHER of the Common Era. He founded a school of philosophy, Neoplatonism, which was a major influence on both late-classical pagan philosophy and early-Christian thought. By means of thinkers such as St. Augustine (354–430), Boethius (480–524), and Pseudo-Dionysius (fl. c. 500), Neoplatonism entered deeply into the fabric of medieval philosophy and theology.

Plotinus was born in Egypt and educated in Alexandria, where he studied for eleven years under the distinguished pagan philosopher Ammonius Saccas. Following an abortive attempt to travel to Mesopotamia to study with Persian and Indian philosophers, Plotinus settled in Rome. There he opened a highly successful school and wrote a series of fifty-four tracts that were later edited by his pupil Porphyry into six books, each with nine sections, and titled *Enneads* (*Nines*). Faithful to his mystical, spirit-centered philosophy, Plotinus was a celibate vegetarian who ate sparingly, meditated frequently, and took little interest in worldly matters. "He was ashamed," Porphyry said, "that his soul had a body."

Plotinus's Neoplatonism was basically a fusion of a souped-up, theologized Platonism with dabs of Aristotelianism, Stoicism, and other ancient philosophies mixed in. Taking hints from Plato's writings, Plotinus crafted an elaborate theological superstructure that viewed the physical universe as the result of a series of emanations from the ultimate Reality, which he called *the One*—an eternal, unchanging, immaterial, unknowable, and absolutely unitary Reality. From the One emanates another divine principle, Mind (*nous*), the source of the eternal Platonic Forms. From Mind emanates Soul, which gives rise to time, individual souls, and the physical world. Like Plato, Plotinus believed that the body is the prison of the soul. The purpose of life is to return to the One by living a life of wisdom, virtue, and self-denial. For most people, salvation will be a process that requires many additional reincarnations. Good and holy souls, however, will permanently merge with the One, thereby losing all personal identity. As Plotinus lay dying, his last words were: "Now I shall endeavor to make that which is divine in me rise up to that which is divine in the universe."

In this leaf from a French illuminated manuscript of Augustine's *City of God*, c. 1475–80, Porphyry and Plotinus discuss the purification of the soul.

SEE ALSO Mind-Body Dualism (c. 380 BCE), Aristotle Enrolls in the Academy (c. 367 BCE), Augustine's Conversion (386), *The Consolation of Philosophy* (524)

AUGUSTINE'S CONVERSION

Augustine of Hippo (354–430)

AUGUSTINE'S *CONFESSIONS* (C. 400) is one of the enduring and unique masterpieces of Western literature and religion. Part confession, part spiritual autobiography, it is cast in the form of an extended prayer, addressed entirely to God but meant to be overheard by us, his readers. It tells a remarkable story about a remarkable man.

Aurelius Augustinus was born in the Roman colony of Thagaste, in what is now eastern Algeria. His mother, Monica, was a devout Christian, but his father, Patricius, was a pagan. A precocious boy, Augustine rose to become a prominent teacher of rhetoric attached to the imperial court in Milan. As a young man, Augustine struggled with both his sexuality (he long kept a mistress and had a son out of wedlock) and his beliefs. For many years, Augustine was an adherent of Manichaeism, a Persian religion centered on a dualistic mythology in which the cosmos is locked in a battle between good (a spiritual world) and evil (a corrupt material world). When Augustine moved from Africa to Italy, he abandoned Manichaeism, switching first to a form of Skepticism and later to Neoplatonism. Largely through the influence of the bishop of Milan, St. Ambrose, Augustine converted to Christianity.

The climactic moment of final conversion is vividly recounted in the *Confessions*. In the summer of 386, as he lay weeping in an agony of indecision under a fig tree in a garden in Milan, Augustine thought he heard children chanting *tolle, lege* ("pick up and read"). He rose, opened a copy of Paul's *Letter to the Romans*, and read the first passage he saw: "But put ye on the Lord Jesus Christ, and make not provision for the flesh, to fulfil the lusts thereof." The following Easter, Augustine and his fifteen-year-old son, Adeodatus, walked naked into the baptismal pool at Milan cathedral and were clothed in white by St. Ambrose when they emerged.

Shortly thereafter, Augustine returned to North Africa, where he later became bishop of Hippo and a prolific writer. (His *The City of God* of 426 is the most important book of the Christian era to the high Middle Ages; primarily a work of theology, it had a profound influence on the course of philosophy.) Gifted with both a powerful mind and a brilliant literary style, Augustine—who was canonized after his death—created a synthesis of Christian thought that made him (in St. Jerome's words) "the second founder of the Christian faith."

> Gifted with both a powerful mind and a brilliant literary style, Augustine created a synthesis of Christian thought.

SEE ALSO Neoplatonism (c. 250)

ORIGINS OF CHAN/ ZEN BUDDHISM

Bodhidharma (fl. c. 550)

WESTERNERS HAVE LONG BEEN FASCINATED by Zen Buddhism, the Japanese version of what is known in China as Chan Buddhism. In some ways, Chan/Zen is a fusion of Daoist and Buddhist ideas. According to Chinese tradition, the founder of Chan Buddhism was an Indian (or possibly Persian) missionary named Bodhidharma, who came to China around 520 CE. In Chinese art, Bodhidharma is invariably depicted as a heavy-set, scowling, bearded monk. According to one story, Emperor Wu, a devoted Buddhist who gave generously to Buddhist causes, requested an interview with Bodhidharma shortly after the latter arrived in China. Wu asked Bodhidharma how much karmic merit flowed from his gifts. The dour monk replied "No merit at all!" He went on to explain that no merit derives from reading or meditation or good works; all that matters is direct insight into the "empty" unitary character of Reality.

> Zen Buddhists believe that all persons have a pure Buddha-nature. The trick, they claim, is to realize it.

Spurned by the shocked emperor, Bodhidharma traveled north to the Shaolin Monastery on Mt. Shaoshi, where he is said to have spent nine years meditating with his face to a wall. More than six centuries after

Bodhidharma's death, Chan Buddhism was introduced to Japan by a Japanese Buddhist, Master Eisai (1141–1215), who had studied it in China.

Zen Buddhists believe that all persons have a pure Buddha-nature. The trick, they claim, is to realize it. Everything in Zen is geared toward achieving a higher state of consciousness, a sudden flash of insight into the nondual, unitary nature of ultimate Reality. The trouble is that words and concepts get in the way. For this reason, Zen masters use a variety of techniques designed to break the grip of reason and logic on students' minds and help them attain enlightenment. These include *koans* (brief, often illogical sayings such as "What is the sound of one hand clapping?"), *mondos* (puzzling question-and-answer sessions), and *haikus* (short poems aimed at overcoming "I" and "not-I" dualities). Occasionally a Zen teacher will respond to a conventional-minded question by whacking a student or tossing them bodily out of a room. The Zen ideal of a mystical, unitive state of consciousness has had a profound impact on many aspects of Chinese and Japanese culture, including martial arts, painting, architecture, gardening, and tea ceremonies.

SEE ALSO The Four Noble Truths (c. 525 BCE)

THE CONSOLATION
OF PHILOSOPHY

Boethius (c. 480–524)

ANICIUS BOETHIUS WAS THE LAST GREAT Roman philosopher, and
arguably the most important philosopher in the Christian West between St.
Augustine (354–430) and St. Anselm (c. 1033–1109). Born into a powerful

"Boethius Takes Counsel of Dame Philosophy," an allegorical miniature from
a fifteenth-century French manuscript of *The Consolation of Philosophy*.

Roman family with a long Christian lineage, Boethius received a classical education and became a prolific author, writing a number of important works on logic, music, arithmetic, and theology, in addition to many commentaries and translations. Fluent in Greek, Boethius set himself the task of translating the complete works of Plato and Aristotle into Latin. Had he succeeded, the whole course of Western civilization might well have been altered. Unfortunately, Boethius became entangled in politics, rose to high office, and was suspected by the Gothic emperor Theodoric of being part of a conspiracy to plot his downfall. Boethius managed to translate only the logical works of Aristotle before he was imprisoned, tortured, and executed. Soon, virtually all knowledge of Plato and Aristotle—except for the logical writings Boethius translated—became lost to the West as Western Europe slipped into the chaos of the Dark Ages.

During his imprisonment, Boethius wrote his most famous book, *The Consolation of Philosophy*; it has always puzzled scholars, because although Boethius was a devout Christian there isn't a trace of Christianity in the book. Instead, Boethius turned to the Greek philosophers he loved for wisdom and comfort in his final days.

British historian Edward Gibbon described *Consolation* as a "golden volume," and so it is to all who love the lucid and serene spirit of the ancient Greek philosophers. Written as a dialogue between Boethius and his "nurse," Philosophy, it is the story of a man's healing journey from sorrow and depression to acceptance and recovered understanding. Its central theme is that happiness does not lie in riches, fame, or power, but in wisdom and virtue, and that perfect happiness consists in life forever with God, who is the absolute and all-sufficient good that satisfies the yearnings of the human heart. Boethius's *Consolation* was one of the most popular books of the Middle Ages. Through it and his translations of and commentaries on Aristotle's logical works, a living echo of ancient Greek wisdom survived the collapse of classical civilization.

SEE ALSO Neoplatonism (c. 250), *Nicomachean Ethics* (c. 330 BCE)

MONISM

Shankara (c. 700–c. 750 or c. 788–c. 820)

DURING THE DARK AGES IN EUROPE, philosophy flourished in India. Some of India's greatest thinkers lived during this period, including Shankara, one of the main exponents of Advaita Vedanta Hinduism.

Little is known for certain about Shankara, though legends abound. Supposedly he was a Brahmin born in the village of Kalady, in southwestern India. As a youth, Shankara dedicated himself to a studious and ascetic life. He traveled widely around India, founding monasteries, engaging in debates with other Indian philosophers, and encouraging religious reform. His major writings include commentaries on the Bhagavad Gita, the principal Upanishads, and the *Brahma Sutras*. It is believed that he died at the young age of thirty-two while traveling in the foothills of the Himalayas.

Advaita Vedanta is a form of Hinduism that asserts the absolute oneness of ultimate reality, a view known as monism. (*Advaita* means "not-two.") Shankara believed that the world we perceive through the senses is *maya*, or illusion. It is an appearance of Brahman, the one true reality, which is pure consciousness and pure bliss. In fact, Shankara argues, terms like "consciousness" and "bliss" are not adequate descriptions of Brahman, because Brahman is so unitary and simple that it has no attributes whatsoever. No human concepts apply to it at all. The goal of human existence is liberation (*moksha*), which occurs when we realize that our highest and deepest self (Ātman) is identical with Brahman, the ultimate reality. No amount of prayer, meditation, good works, or religious devotion can result in liberation. We must replace ignorance (*avidya*) with wisdom (*vidya*) by realizing the oneness of all reality.

Later adherents of Vedanta, such as the South Indian theologian and philosopher Ramanuja (d. 1137), objected that Shankara's Advaita approach was overly intellectualized and gave too little importance to devotion (*bhakti*) as a path to liberation. They also questioned Shankara's claim that Brahman has no properties. If, as Shankara claims, Brahman has no parts, doesn't it have the property of lacking parts? And what about negative properties like "not being a horse"? Doesn't that property literally apply to Brahman? These are the sorts of debates that continue today in Indian philosophy between supporters and critics of Advaita Vedanta.

> Shankara believed that the world we perceive through the senses is *maya*, or illusion. It is an appearance of Brahman, the one true reality.

SEE ALSO The *Bhagavad Gita* (c. 400 BCE), *Ethics* (1677)

THE ONTOLOGICAL ARGUMENT

Anselm of Canterbury (c. 1033–1109)

ANSELM IS WIDELY CONSIDERED the most important Christian philosopher and theologian of the eleventh century. He was born to a noble family in Aosta, a beautiful town in the foothills of the Italian Alps. In his mid-twenties he became a Benedictine monk in the monastery of Bec in western France. In 1093 he became the archbishop of Canterbury, where he clashed frequently with English kings and spent much of his tenure in exile. He is buried in Canterbury Cathedral and was later canonized.

In his work the *Monologion* (1076), Anselm drew on premises taken from Christian Platonism to offer a densely argued proof of God's existence and His chief attributes. In the *Proslogion* (1077–78), he offers a much shorter proof, his now-celebrated ontological argument for God's existence. The argument is often included in introductory philosophy texts and has produced an enormous secondary literature. Although most philosophers today reject the argument as unsound, many great philosophers have defended it.

There is a good deal of controversy about how exactly the argument should be construed, but the gist of it is this: God, by definition, is the greatest conceivable being. If God were merely an idea in our heads, He would not be the greatest conceivable being because then we could imagine a greater being—namely one that exists in reality as well as in our heads. Therefore God, the most perfect conceivable being, actually exists.

In the ongoing debate over the soundness of the ontological argument, some have questioned whether Anselm is entitled to assume that existence is a "great-making property," or that we know by definition that God is the most perfect possible being, or that God is even a possible being. Shortly after Anselm published his argument, a French monk named Gaunilo contended that Anselm's reasoning must be faulty because if it worked, we could prove the existence of all kinds of things that we know do not exist, such as the most perfect conceivable island. Whether the argument is ultimately successful or not, it is a wonderful argument to think about, because it touches on so many deep questions of language and metaphysics.

A woodcut depicting Anselm of Canterbury from the *Nuremberg Chronicle*, an illustrated historical encyclopedia published in Nuremberg, Germany, in 1493.

SEE ALSO *Outlines of Pyrrhonism* (c. 200), Neoplatonism (c. 250), The Five Ways (c. 1265)

THE GREAT MEDIEVAL SYNTHESIS

Thomas Aquinas (c. 1225–74)

THOMAS AQUINAS IS WIDELY RECOGNIZED as the greatest Christian philosopher and theologian of the Middle Ages. His greatest achievement was to fuse the philosophy of Aristotle with Christian doctrine in a vast synthesis of impressive power and scope. For over seven hundred years, Aquinas has been a leading figure in Roman Catholic thought and education, and he has been a major influence on Western thought generally, particularly in the fields of ethics and law.

Aquinas was born in Roccasecca, in Southern Italy, in 1225. After studying at the University of Naples, he joined the Dominican order and devoted the remainder of his life to teaching, preaching, and writing. Blessed with a clear mind and a near-photographic memory, Aquinas wrote prodigiously on a wide range of philosophical and theological topics. The two most important sources of his philosophical work are *Summa contra gentiles* (written 1259–65) and *Summa theologica* (written 1265–74). Aquinas stopped writing following a vision in late 1273, saying that compared to the things that had been revealed to him, all that he had written "appears to be as so much straw." He died in 1274 as he was traveling to the Council of Lyons and was declared a saint in 1323.

Like his famous teacher, Albertus Magnus (c. 1200–1280), Aquinas was a huge fan of Aristotle. However, harmonizing Aristotle with Christian teaching wasn't easy. Aristotle was a pagan who taught that the universe was not created, that there is no personal survival after death, and that God is unaware of the world's existence. By virtue of some judicious pruning, Aquinas was able to show that substantial portions of Aristotle's thought could be integrated into a Christian framework.

The Christian-Aristotelian synthesis Aquinas created depended on the strength of the philosophical foundations Aquinas built for his theological superstructure. Aquinas had great confidence in the power of reason to grasp fundamental moral truths and to prove the existence of God, His perfect nature, and the immortality of the soul. Following Aquinas's death, Christian thinkers such as John Duns Scotus (c. 1265–1308) and William of Ockham (c. 1287–1347) began to attack some or all of these philosophical underpinnings, raising doubts in many people's minds about the viability of Aquinas's synthesis.

An engraving of St. Thomas Aquinas by Michel Natalis after Abraham van Diepenbeeck, c. 1620–68. He holds a monstrance in one hand, and a feather quill in the other.

SEE ALSO: *Nicomachean Ethics* (c. 330 BCE), Ockham's Razor (c. 1320)

THE FIVE WAYS

Thomas Aquinas (c. 1225–74)

THOMAS AQUINAS is perhaps best known for his five arguments for God's existence, the so-called Five Ways, outlined in his masterwork, *Summa theologica* (written 1265–74). Indeed, these are among the most famous arguments in the entire history of philosophy.

The first three arguments share a similar pattern. The argument from motion claims that there must be an ultimate cause of motion—an unmoved mover—to explain why anything is in motion now. The argument from causation asserts that there must be a first cause to explain why there are chains of causes and effects. And the argument from necessity claims that there must be a necessary being to explain the existence of dependent beings—that is, things whose existence is explained by the causal activity of other beings.

The Fourth Way, the argument from degree, argues that there must be a perfect being that possesses maximal goodness and reality to explain why there are things that possess lesser amounts of goodness and reality. The Fifth Way is a version of the traditional argument from design (based on evidence of divine design in the natural world). It claims that an intelligent designer must exist to account for why things that lack awareness and intelligence (such as plants) often behave in seemingly intelligent and goal-directed ways.

Many scholars believe that the Third Way, the argument from necessity, may be the strongest of the bunch. Aquinas assumes that everything that exists must have a sufficient reason why it exists. In other words, there cannot be any brute facts—things that exist but have absolutely no reason why they exist. If there is no necessary being and the universe consists entirely of dependent beings, it seems that there'd be no sufficient reason why the universe exists; its existence would be simply a brute fact. It's plausible to suppose that the only way everything could have an explanation is if God explains Himself (He is a self-existent, self-explanatory being) and the existence of the universe. Perhaps the weakest point in this argument is Aquinas's assumption that there cannot be any brute facts. Do we know this for a fact? Many critics of Aquinas's Five Ways would say no.

> Aquinas assumes that everything that exists must have a sufficient reason why it exists. In other words, there cannot be any brute facts.

SEE ALSO The Ontological Argument (1078)

NATURAL LAW

Thomas Aquinas (c. 1225–74)

ONE OF THOMAS AQUINAS'S most enduring legacies is the theory of ethics he developed. Aquinas taught that all normal, adult human beings grasp certain basic moral truths. Aquinas calls these basic, universally knowable ethical principles "natural law."

The idea of natural law goes back to the ancient Greeks, particularly to the Stoics, who taught that there is a higher law than the moral and legal codes created by human beings. This higher law emanates from God, is binding at all times and places, and is self-evident to all who have full use of their reason. The Stoics called this higher law *natural law* because it is rooted in basic facts about human nature (e.g., that children require a lengthy period of care and education) and also because people come to know it by nature and do not need to be taught it. Aquinas took over this Stoic idea of natural law, combined it with a largely Aristotelian account of the virtues, and developed it into a full-blown theory of ethics.

> Natural law is that set of basic moral principles, rooted in human nature and divine ordinance, which can be known by the natural light of reason.

Aquinas distinguishes four kinds of law. Eternal law is God's providential governance of the entire universe. Human law consists of all the enacted rules in human legal systems. Divine law is comprised of all God's commands that can be known only through revelation. Finally, the natural law is that set of basic moral principles, rooted in human nature and divine ordinance, which can be known by the natural light of reason.

Aquinas's account of natural law became standard in Catholic moral teaching and was widely accepted by non-Catholic ethicists prior to about 1800. When the US Declaration of Independence speaks of "self-evident" moral truths and "Laws of Nature and of Nature's God," it is echoing this natural law tradition. Many people now question whether moral norms can reliably be read off from appeals to "human nature" or what is "natural," as some natural law theorists appear to do. In modern liberal societies, many acts that were once widely condemned as "unnatural" (e.g., use of contraceptives and artificial insemination) aren't generally viewed as unethical. Nevertheless, natural law theory is still a fairly widely accepted approach to ethics today.

SEE ALSO Stoicism (c. 300 BCE), Universal Moral Law (51 BCE)

OCKHAM'S RAZOR

William of Ockham (c. 1287–c. 1347)

WILLIAM OF OCKHAM was the most influential philosopher of the four-teenth century. Curiously, however, the idea for which he is most famous, the principle of theoretical simplicity known as *Ockham's razor*, was never endorsed by him in the way it is usually formulated.

Ockham was born in the village of Ockham, not far from London. After joining the Franciscan order in his teens, he studied at Oxford and was on the verge of becoming a regent master when his career was cut short by an accusation of heresy. Ockham spent four years at the papal court in Avignon trying to clear his name, but was finally forced to flee when he and the head of the Franciscan order, Michael of Cesena, butted heads with Pope John XXII on the issue of evangelical poverty. Both Franciscans were excommu-nicated and spent the rest of their lives in Munich under the protection of Emperor Louis IV of Bavaria, who was at war with the pope.

Though he was a great admirer of Aristotle, Ockham's central aim was to free Christianity from what he saw as the corrupting influences of Greek philosophy. Ockham denied that God's existence or infinite perfection could be proved by reason. He also denied that reason can demonstrate the soul's immortality or the existence of free will. Moreover, he completely rejected Aquinas's natural law approach to ethics, arguing instead that morality depends entirely upon the will or the commands of God. These views are consistent with Ockham's overriding concern to widen the gap between theology and philosophy and to protect the omnipotence and freedom of God from any human-concocted notions that might limit them.

One of the tools Ockham uses to achieve these ends is the principle popularly known as Ockham's razor. The standard formulation of the principle—that "entities are not to be multiplied beyond necessity"—is not found in Ockham's works. He *did* say that "plurality is not to be posited without necessity," which amounts to much the same thing. The core idea is that, all other things being equal, simpler theories and explanations are to be preferred. Understood in this sense, Ockham's razor is a widely accepted methodological principle in both philosophy and science.

The core idea is that, all other things being equal, simpler theories and explanations are to be preferred.

SEE ALSO The Great Medieval Synthesis (c. 1265)

THE RENAISSANCE BEGINS

THE RENAISSANCE PRODUCED few first-rank philosophers, but it created the conditions for the birth of modern philosophy in the age that followed. Beginning in Italy around the 1350s, the Renaissance marks the rebirth of classical literature and a renewed sense of the value and joys of earthly existence. Whereas the characteristic notes of the Middle Ages were self-abnegation, otherworldliness, preoccupation with sin, and fear of divine punishment, the spirit of the Renaissance was one of discovery, optimism, and belief in the dignity of human nature.

The Renaissance — together with the Reformation — opened the door to greater freedom of thought, particularly in Protestant countries.

Several things occurred during the Renaissance that set the stage for the genesis of modern philosophy. One was the recovery of the writings of Plato and other Greek and Roman philosophers. This helped to reduce the dominance of Aristotle on the European mind and offered new avenues for philosophical thought. Another important event was the decline of medieval Scholasticism. Thinkers like Petrarch and Erasmus attacked what they saw as the arid intellectualism, hair-splitting logic, and excessively theoretical focus of thirteenth-century Scholastics such as Aquinas and Duns Scotus. For Petrarch, the whole point of philosophy was to teach the art of living happily and well, and he condemned Scholasticism for losing sight of this practical purpose. A third significant development was the rise of modern science. Discoveries by such sixteenth-century giants as Nicolaus Copernicus, Johannes Kepler, and Galileo Galilei served to further weaken the authority of Aristotle and provided thinkers like Francis Bacon and René Descartes with a new evidence-based paradigm of reliable inquiry.

Finally, the Renaissance—together with the Reformation—opened the door to greater freedom of thought, particularly in Protestant countries. In England, for example, the works of Michel de Montaigne and Niccolò Machiavelli were widely read, despite the fact that both writers were on the Catholic Church's "Index of Prohibited Books." The Italian philosopher Giordano Bruno lived and wrote freely in England for several years, though he was later burned as a heretic by the Inquisition in Rome. Decades later, Descartes and Spinoza were able to reside and publish largely unmolested in Holland. Such freedoms would have been unthinkable prior to the Renaissance and Reformation.

SEE ALSO The Humanist Ideal (c. 1520), *The Prince* (1532), The Birth of Modern Science (1543)

UTOPIA

Sir Thomas More (1478–1535)

THOMAS MORE is among the most dynamic figures of the Renaissance. Humanist, historian, statesman, martyr, and saint, More is best remembered as the author of *Utopia*, a kind of philosophical novel (in Latin) about a fictional island in the South Atlantic. In Greek, the word *utopia* means

Detail of a page from an original 1516 edition of More's *Utopia*, published in Flanders, showing a map of the island of Utopia.

"nowhere place" while *eutopia* means "happy place." Like Plato's *Republic*, on which it is partly modeled, More's *Utopia* is offered as a blueprint of what a rational and just state would be like. It also held up a satirical mirror to the follies and vices of the Christian Europe of More's time.

In More's tale, Utopia is a crescent-shaped island 500 miles long by 200 miles wide. On the island are 54 identical-looking cities, each with out-lying farms. There is no private property and no money. (There is gold, but it is despised and used only for chamber pots and prisoners' chains.) The people live in large, identical state-owned households and eat their meals in big cafeterias. Clothing is simple and sturdy, and all citizens dress pretty much alike. There are no idlers and everyone who can work works, but the workday is only six hours long so there is plenty of time for leisure and cultural activities. Besides working in the fields, every citizen learns a craft, such as shoemaking. These craft-products are stockpiled and offered free to whoever needs them. The government is a form of representative democracy, punishments are mild, and wars are fought only for self-defense or to punish aggressors.

Most Utopians worship an ineffable higher power they call "the father of all." Other religions are tolerated, though civil penalties are imposed on those who deny the existence of God or the immortality of the soul. Priests are elected by popular vote, and some priests are women. As for morality, Utopians reject fasting and other forms of self-denial; "No kind of pleasure is forbidden, provided harm does not come of it." As one would expect, there are many features of More's *Utopia* that strike modern readers as less than ideal. But it cannot be denied that in many ways More was far ahead of his time.

SEE ALSO Plato's *Republic* (c. 380 BCE)

THE HUMANIST IDEAL

Desiderius Erasmus (c. 1466–1536)

RENAISSANCE HUMANISTS WERE NOT, as a rule, secular humanists. They were Christian humanists who celebrated the educational and formative values of "humane letters" (that is, the Greek and Roman classics) while remaining in the Christian fold. The greatest figure of Renaissance Christian humanism was the Dutch scholar Desiderius Erasmus.

Erasmus was born out of wedlock in Rotterdam, Holland. After receiving an excellent grounding in Latin classics in Deventer, Erasmus was orphaned when the plague killed his parents. He was reluctantly persuaded by his guardians to become an Augustinian monk. After six years he left the monastery, studied at the University of Paris, and became an itinerant scholar. Many of Erasmus's works, including *Adagia* (1500), *Colloquia* (1518), and *Encomium Moriae* (*The Praise of Folly*) (1511), became best sellers.

As a humanist, Erasmus endlessly sang the praises of a classical education and of Ciceronian over medieval Latin. As a Christian, he strongly disliked Scholastic theology and favored a return to a simpler, less dogmatic form of Christian piety. He was such a staunch supporter of church reform that many expected him to join Martin Luther's Protestant revolt when it broke out in 1517. Erasmus's answer came in 1524 when he published *De Libero Arbitrio . . .* (*On Free Will . . .*), directly challenging Luther's core teachings of divine predestination, total depravity, and God's absolute sovereignty. It is widely considered to be Erasmus's most important philosophical work.

In addition to citing reams of quotations from the Bible and fathers of the Church supporting the idea of free will, Erasmus argues that the denial of human freedom is inconsistent with the idea of a just and loving God. How could a just God punish us for sins we could not help committing? If God completely determines all our thoughts and actions, must he not be the ultimate author of sin? How is being a puppet on God's string consistent with Christian ideals of human dignity? In 1525, Luther responded in *De Servo Arbitrio* (*On the Bondage of the Will*), an uncompromising denial of free will and a defense of God's absolute sovereignty. Most of Luther's contemporaries thought he won the argument.

An engraved portrait of Erasmus at work by his contemporary, Albrecht Dürer, 1526.

SEE ALSO The Renaissance Begins (c. 1350)

1532

THE PRINCE

Niccolò Machiavelli (1469–1527)

MACHIAVELLI'S *THE PRINCE* (written in 1513 but not published until 1532) is the bible of power politics. Reviled by many as a godless and amoral cynic, praised by others as a far-seeing prophet who dared to tell the truth about power, Machiavelli remains a towering figure with whom all students of political thought must come to terms.

Machiavelli was born in Florence, the son of a moderately prosperous lawyer. From a young age, his great passions were the Latin classics (particularly the Roman historians) and politics. For fourteen years he served as a diplomat and army organizer under the Florentine republic. In 1512, the republic was overthrown by the armies of Pope Julius II; Machiavelli was captured, tortured, and exiled. It was during his years of enforced retirement that he wrote his two great works of political theory, *The Prince* and *Discourses* (written c. 1517, published 1531).

The Prince is a practical manual on how to keep and preserve power in the world of realpolitik. Machiavelli believed that sound political thinking must begin with the recognition that all men are essentially selfish, acquisitive, and vicious. Many previous political thinkers had written utopian fantasies or sermonized about the moral duties of Christian rulers. Machiavelli considered all of that a waste of ink. In the real world of Italian politics that he knew, a sheepish prince would quickly be eaten up by his wolfish neighbors.

Some have suggested that *The Prince* is simply a piece of descriptive, value-free analysis of how to play the game of power politics successfully. In fact, the work reflects an ethic that looks back to the ancient Roman ideal of *virtus*—masculinity, strength of character, courage, boldness—but taken a step further. Effective rulers possess what Machiavelli calls *virtù*—meaning they are prepared to set aside considerations of morality or religion whenever the safety of the state or the imperatives of power demand it. Like Nietzsche (1844–1900), Machiavelli rejected the Christian virtues of gentleness, meekness, humility, and contempt for worldly things. Given the natural wickedness of man, this simply makes the weak the prey of the strong. He much preferred the sterner virtues of courage, energy, strength, boldness, and crafty intelligence.

In the real world of Italian politics that [Machiavelli] knew, a sheepish prince would quickly be eaten up by his wolfish neighbors.

SEE ALSO The Renaissance Begins (c. 1350), The Revaluation of Values (1887)

THE BIRTH OF MODERN SCIENCE

NOTHING HAS HAD A GREATER IMPACT on the course of Western philosophy than the rise of modern science, which can be said to have begun with the publication of Nicolaus Copernicus's great work, *On the Revolutions of the Celestial Spheres*, in 1543. The scientific revolution, spanning the fifteenth to seventeenth centuries and brought about by men such as Copernicus, Kepler, Bacon, Galileo, Descartes, and Newton, led to the overthrow of the medieval worldview.

Prior to the scientific revolution, the reigning paradigm of Scholastic Aristotelianism was so hidebound by tradition and respect for authority that it produced little in the way of original thought. The rise of modern science led to a new birth of intellectual freedom. Philosophers such as Descartes and Hobbes threw off the straightjacket of ossified Scholasticism and struck out in bold new directions. Philosophy was no longer seen as simply the handmaid of theology. It had a charter and an agenda of its own.

> The rise of modern science led to a new birth of intellectual freedom.

The scientific revolution also led to a sharper separation of science and philosophy. Increasingly, philosophers left scientific problems to the scientists and focused on what Bertrand Russell (1872–1970) called the "No Man's Land" of speculative thought, on which definite knowledge is difficult or impossible to attain. Philosophy came to be regarded as what John Locke called an "under-laborer" for science, charged with clearing obstacles and "rubbish" that impeded its growth. The remarkable success science had achieved through observation and experimentation inspired the growth of British empiricism.

On the continent, the mathematical and deductive aspects of modern science fueled the rise of rationalism in mathematically oriented thinkers like Descartes and Spinoza. The mechanical explanations of natural phenomena favored by scientists such as Galileo, Robert Boyle (1627–91), and Isaac Newton (1642–1727) led to atomistic philosophies of nature in thinkers like Hobbes and Descartes. The heady triumphs of natural science inspired philosophers such as Hume to apply "the experimental method of reasoning" to "moral subjects" such as psychology and sociology. Finally, science has contributed to a steady growth of secularism among philosophers in the modern era. Whereas prior to the scientific revolution, nearly all Western philosophers were theists, today a clear majority of them are naturalists. The growth of science, no doubt, is a major reason for the shift.

SEE ALSO The Renaissance Begins (c. 1350), The Enlightenment Begins (1620), The Father of Modern Philosophy (1637)

1620

THE ENLIGHTENMENT BEGINS

Francis Bacon (1561–1626)

IMMANUEL KANT (1724–1804) famously defined the Enlightenment as "man's release from his self-incurred tutelage" and declared its motto to be "*Sapere aude!* [Dare to know!] Have courage to use your own understanding."

The Enlightenment of the seventeenth and eighteenth centuries was a complex intellectual and cultural movement, but several salient themes stand out. These include a rejection of authoritarianism and gloomy superstition in matters of belief; faith in the power of reason and science to discover truth and to improve the human condition; a commitment to toleration, political freedom, and human rights; and a belief in progress through reason, science, and education. Leading Enlightenment figures include Francis Bacon, René Descartes, Baruch Spinoza, John Locke, Isaac Newton, Voltaire, Denis Diderot, David Hume, Benjamin Franklin, and Thomas Jefferson.

Scholars debate when the Enlightenment began, but a good case can be made that it started with the publication of Francis Bacon's *Novum Organum* in 1620. There, Bacon attacks medieval science, logic, and philosophy, arguing that the only reliable way of forming beliefs about the natural world is through patient scientific induction. Doing such rigorous empirical science is difficult, in part because of certain biases and preconceptions that affect our observations and distort our inferences. Bacon calls these distorting factors "idols," and he identifies four main varieties: idols of the tribe (errors that flow from inherent tendencies in the human mind, such as wishful thinking), idols of the cave (errors that derive from one's own personal biases, temperament, and predispositions), idols of the marketplace (errors that stem from confusions of language), and idols of the theater (errors due to uncritical acceptance of false philosophies of the past).

Title page for a 1645 edition of Bacon's *Novum Organum* published in Leiden, Holland. *Organum* references *Organon*, Aristotle's works on logic (the word means *instrument* or *tool* in Greek). The Latin phrase under the ship, *Multi pertransibunt & augebitur scientia*, translates as "Many will travel and knowledge will be increased."

The heyday of the Enlightenment lasted until the emergence of Romanticism in the late eighteenth century, but in many ways we continue to be children of the Enlightenment. Though faith in progress, science, and reason may have waned somewhat since the heady days of Locke and Jefferson, belief in toleration, political freedom, and human rights has grown, and few today would question the value of independent judgment and "critical thinking" in forming one's beliefs.

SEE ALSO The Birth of Modern Science (1543)

THE FATHER OF MODERN PHILOSOPHY

René Descartes (1596–1650)

THE SEVENTEENTH CENTURY marks the birth of modern philosophy. The most important figure in the transition from medieval to modern philosophy was the French philosopher, scientist, and mathematician René Descartes. With him, philosophy made a fresh start.

Descartes was born in La Haye en Touraine (renamed Descartes in 1967) in central France. After receiving a fine liberal arts education at the Jesuit Collège Royal Henry-Le-Grand at La Flèche, he traveled widely and briefly served as a soldier, desiring to learn from "the great book of the world," as he later said. As a young man, Descartes dedicated himself to the monumental task of constructing a universal science, built on the model of mathematics. Coming from a well-to-do family, he was able to pursue this goal single-mindedly, without the distraction of needing to earn a living. He lived a quiet, scholarly life, in accordance with his personal motto: "He has lived well who has hidden well."

Descartes believed that philosophy was stuck in a rut and could never achieve solid results until it became as rigorous as mathematics. In his classic *Discourse on the Method* (1637), he laid down four rules for conducting careful intellectual inquiry. The first of these was to accept nothing as true that one does not clearly and distinctly perceive to be true.

Descartes is rightly called "the father of modern philosophy" for several reasons. First, he broke sharply from medieval philosophy and proposed a new model for doing philosophy, one founded on clear definitions and rigorous reasoning from indisputable starting points. Second, he shifted the main focus of philosophy from questions of being or existence to questions of knowledge, thus initiating what is known as the "epistemological turn" in early modern philosophy. Third, Descartes exalted the power of human reason, claiming that all sorts of fundamental truths about reality could be discovered just by thinking, without the aid of the senses. In so doing, he launched a powerful movement in philosophy known as "rationalism." Finally, he rejected the dense, jargon-ridden writing style of the medieval Scholastics. Descartes wrote

> [Descartes] shifted the main focus of philosophy from questions of being or existence to questions of knowledge.

elegantly and clearly, setting an admirable pattern that most European philosophers followed until the close of the eighteenth century.

SEE ALSO *Meditations on First Philosophy* (1641), *Ethics* (1677)

MEDITATIONS ON FIRST PHILOSOPHY

René Descartes (1596–1650)

René Descartes in his study, a portrait created in 1687–91
by Dutch engraver Cornelis A. Hellemans.

DESCARTES'S *MEDITATIONS ON FIRST PHILOSOPHY* (1641) is one of the undisputed classics of philosophy. More than 375 years after it was first published, it remains one of the most widely read texts in introductory philosophy courses. Part of the charm of the *Meditations* is its personal touch. It is an existential quest, rather than a dry treatise. Its basic narrative arc is that of a man who thinks his way from a state of doubt and confusion to one of triumphant and secure self-understanding.

The goals of the *Meditations* are incredibly ambitious: to determine if anything can be known with complete certainty; to refute skepticism and materialism; to provide new and secure foundations for science, philosophy, and theology; to replace Aristotle's philosophy of nature; and to prove the existence of God and the immortality of the soul. The book begins with Descartes's famous "method of doubt": to doubt everything except what is absolutely certain and indubitable. Over the course of the six meditations, readers encounter some of the most iconic memes in all of philosophy. Could our senses systematically deceive us? Might life be simply a dream? Could what we call reality actually be a cruel hoax perpetrated by an "evil genius"? Could even reason and logic be deceptive? Is my own existence the one rock-solid certainty ("I think, therefore I am")? Can God's existence be proved simply by reflecting on the idea of God? Would a good and truthful God allow human beings to be systematically deceived about the nature of reality? Are human beings simply material creatures, or do we have a nonphysical soul that is distinct from the body and capable of surviving after the body dies?

Few philosophers today believe that Descartes was successful in proving his desired conclusions. Most are unconvinced, in particular, by his arguments for the existence of God and an immaterial soul. Nonetheless, the *Meditations* remains one of the enduring classics of philosophy because of the fascinating questions it poses, its readability, and its engaging first-person narrative structure.

SEE ALSO *Outlines of Pyrrhonism* (c. 200), The Father of Modern Philosophy (1637)

LEVIATHAN

Thomas Hobbes (1588–1679)

THOMAS HOBBES'S *LEVIATHAN* is a bold and original work. In his day, Hobbes was widely seen as a dangerous thinker because of his support for materialism, determinism, egoistic psychology, government control of religion, and an all-powerful state. *Leviathan* was a major influence on later English moral and political theory. Among its most influential ideas is that of the social contract as the basis of government.

Hobbes was born in Westport, England, a former village near Malmesbury. After graduating from Oxford, Hobbes became a private tutor in the household of the Earl of Devonshire. In 1640, when his views on absolute royal power became known, Hobbes fled to France for eleven years to avoid possible persecution. There he tutored the future Charles II and wrote a reply to Descartes's *Meditations*. Hobbes returned to England shortly after *Leviathan* was published in 1651. He lived to the ripe age of ninety-one, a fact that he attributed to his nightly habit of singing lustily in bed.

Leviathan is a wide-ranging, lucidly written book that tackles a broad range of philosophical issues. What it is best remembered for today is its account of how society and government are formed. Long ago, Hobbes says, humans lived in small bands without any sort of social organization or government. Hobbes calls this aboriginal condition "the state of nature." Because humans are naturally selfish, violent, and power-hungry, this state of nature was a state of perpetual violence in which most people lived lives that were "solitary, poor, nasty, brutish, and short." To escape this dire condition, people decided to create an organized society with government and laws. They agreed on a "social contract" that vested virtually total power in a king or a small group of rulers. Only if the sovereign possesses near-absolute power, Hobbes argued, can it guarantee peace and security.

Hobbes's notions of the state of nature and the social contract were powerful ideas that sparked a great deal of discussion. Later thinkers, like John Locke (1632–1704) and Jean-Jacques Rousseau (1712–78), offered their own versions of social-contract theory, and today it is widely accepted that just governments rest "on the consent of the governed."

The original edition of Hobbes's *Leviathan*, published in London in 1651, features an elaborate illustration by French engraver Abraham Bosse.

SEE ALSO Human Rights (1689), *The Social Contract* (1762), *A Theory of Justice* (1971), Political Libertarianism (1974)

FREE WILL AND DETERMINISM ARE COMPATIBLE

Thomas Hobbes (1588–1679)

MANY THINKERS IMPRESSED by the march of modern science have claimed that every event in the universe is an inevitable consequence of prior causes. This is a view called "determinism."

On the face of it, determinism seems to rule out any idea of free will. After all, if determinism is true, then all our acts and choices are the inevitable outcome of antecedent causes, some stretching back to before we were born. But if all our acts and choices are necessitated by prior causes, it seems that those acts and choices are not up to us. And if they are not up to us, how can they be free?

Hobbes was one of the first in a long line of modern thinkers who deny that free will is incompatible with determinism. He argued for "compatibilism," the view that determinism is not inconsistent with free will. Hobbes accepted determinism. He thought that since "every act of man's will, and every desire and inclination, proceed from some cause, and that from another cause, in a continual chain (whose first link is in the hand of God, the first of all causes), they proceed from *necessity*." But just because an act is necessitated does not mean that it is not free. A person acts freely if "he finds no stop in doing what he has the will, desire, or inclination to do." In other words, we are "free" if we are able to do as we wish without constraint or impediment. Many acts are free in this sense even if determinism is true.

Many philosophers have challenged Hobbes's definition of "free will." Suppose I hypnotize you and say "When I clap my hands three times, quack like a duck." I clap my hands three times and you say "Quack, quack." You were able to do what you wanted. There was "no stop" in your ability to do what you had "the will, desire, or inclination to do." Yet it seems clear that your act was not free.

Modern compatibilists have come up with a variety of sophisticated responses to criticisms of this sort. Whether any of them succeed is still a matter of lively debate.

[Hobbes] argued for "compatibilism," the view that determinism is not inconsistent with free will.

SEE ALSO Stoicism (c. 300 BCE)

PASCAL'S WAGER

Blaise Pascal (1623–62)

The American intellectual Allan Bloom (1930–92) wrote that "there are two writers who between them shape and set the limits to the minds of educated Frenchmen." One is Descartes, who celebrated the power of reason, and the other is Blaise Pascal, who stressed the limitations of reason and the wretchedness of human beings without God.

Pascal was a universal genius who made important contributions to mathematics, probability theory, and science. Today he is best remembered as the author of two masterpieces of classic French prose: *The Provincial Letters* (1656–57) and the unfinished, posthumously published *Pensées* (*Thoughts*) (1670). Despite its fragmentary condition, the *Pensées* is highly readable and filled with brilliant insights. Its central theme is the paradoxical nature of humanity (at once brutish and angelic) and the weakness of human reason. Left to itself, Pascal argues, reason quickly bogs down in a morass of unintelligibility and doubt. Reason cannot prove God's existence, the soul's immortality, the reality of moral truth, the meaningfulness of existence, or the reliability of the Scriptures. Ultimately, we must trust "the reasons of the heart" rather than reason alone. Only in faith and in divine revelation can we find the answers and the healing we seek.

> In the *Pensées*, Pascal offers his famous "wager argument" [that] it makes sense to "bet" that God exists.

In the *Pensées*, Pascal offers his famous "wager argument" for belief in God: No one can truly know, through reason alone, whether God exists or not. Still, it makes sense to "bet" that God exists because we have everything to gain if He does and little or nothing to lose if He doesn't. If we believe in God, and He exists, we gain eternal happiness and bliss. If we don't believe in God, and He does exist, we risk eternal loss and damnation. Finally, if God doesn't exist, there's no big gain or loss whether we believe that He exists or not. Given these alternatives, the smart thing to do is bet on God, live a religious life, and hope for the best.

Is Pascal's Wager sound? Many philosophers have rejected it with scorn and indignation. Certainly some of his assumptions about the relevant options can be questioned. But if you begin from Pascal's starting points, the argument may be compelling.

SEE ALSO "The Will to Believe" (1897)

ETHICS

Baruch Spinoza (1632–77)

BERTRAND RUSSELL (d. 1970) described the Dutch philosopher Baruch Spinoza as "the noblest and most lovable of the great philosophers." Characteristically, Russell adds: "As a natural consequence, he was considered, during his lifetime and for a century after his death, a man of appalling wickedness." Like many profoundly original thinkers, Spinoza has always attracted fervent critics and admirers.

A portrait of Baruch Spinoza by French engraver Etienne Fessard, c. 1740.

Spinoza was born in Amsterdam into a well-to-do family of Portuguese Jewish merchants. At an early age, he became interested in philosophy and began to have doubts about the religion he'd been taught. When he refused to conform, he was cursed and solemnly excommunicated from the Jewish community and disowned by his family. Thereafter he lived quietly and simply in rented rooms, making ends meet by grinding lenses for glasses and optical instruments. In 1670, he published (anonymously) the *Tractatus Theologico-Politicus*, a critique of conventional religion and a landmark in modern biblical criticism. His major work, *Ethics*, was published in 1677, following his early death from tuberculosis.

The *Ethics* is a remarkable book in both style and substance. Its central idea is that only one reality ("substance") exists, which Spinoza calls "God or Nature." This reality is infinite, eternal, and perfect but is not a personal god in the sense of traditional theism. God has an infinite number of attributes, including thought and extension. The universe is God's body, and what we ordinarily think of as separate "things," like stars, cabbages, and human beings, are simply "modes" of God. The supreme good of human existence is to free ourselves from the bondage of worldly lusts and con-straining emotions and to achieve wisdom and blessedness by identifying ourselves with the infinite, accepting the necessitated course of things, and devoting ourselves to the "intellectual love" of God.

All of this Spinoza claimed to prove with rigorous, airtight reasoning. The *Ethics* is written like a geometry text. It begins with definitions and axioms, and proceeds to prove its numbered conclusions with mathematical exactitude. This makes the *Ethics* a difficult but absorbing book to read. As Spinoza himself said, "all excellent things are as difficult as they are rare."

SEE ALSO Monism (c. 810)

1689

HUMAN RIGHTS

John Locke (1632–1704)

AS HISTORIAN FREDERICK COPLESTON (1907–94) noted, the political writings of John Locke are "a standing disproof of the notion that philosophers are ineffectual." Though considered radical in their day, Locke's core political ideas are now widely accepted. Among these is the idea of human rights.

Locke was born near Bristol, England, and educated at Westminster School and Christ Church, Oxford. For several years, he taught at Christ Church, but most of his life was spent in government service, practicing medicine, and in other nonacademic pursuits. For reasons of health and safety, Locke spent most of the period between 1675 and 1688 in France and Holland. This gave him time to write. His major works include *Two Treatises of Government* (1689), *An Essay Concerning Human Understanding* (1689), *A Letter Concerning Toleration* (1689), and *The Reasonableness of Christianity* (1695).

In the *Two Treatises*, Locke critiques the philosophy of political theorist Robert Filmer (c. 1588–1653), who posited that kings possess a God-given right to rule ("the divine right of kings"). Locke argues that government rests on the consent of the governed. Originally, as Hobbes held, humans lived in a "state of nature" without governments or laws. But Locke's picture of the state of nature is very different from Hobbes's—it isn't a *Hunger Games*–like war of all against all; humans are naturally sociable and rational, and they recognize a binding natural moral law, "the law of nature." This law teaches that all humans are naturally free and equal, and that they possess basic rights to life, freedom, and property that may not be rightfully infringed. These basic, universal, pre-political rights are what the American Declaration of Independence calls "inalienable rights." Today we call them human rights.

Locke famously argues that governments were created when people decided to try to better their lives by leaving the state of nature and forming governments by means of a "social contract." Since the very purpose of governments is to protect basic rights and freedoms, they may be forcibly overthrown (if necessary) whenever there is a flagrant failure to do so. This became a rallying cry in the American Revolution and in many later political movements.

John Locke, depicted in a nineteenth-century illustration.

SEE ALSO Religious Liberty (1689), Natural Law (c. 1270), *Leviathan* (1651), *The Social Contract* (1762), Political Libertarianism (1974)

RELIGIOUS LIBERTY

John Locke (1632–1704)

DESPITE CENTURIES OF ATTACKS on "the civil rights and worldly goods of each other upon pretence of religion" that inevitably resulted in what Locke termed "endless hatreds, rapines, and slaughters," few Europeans in his day believed in any kind of robust religious freedom. Locke's was one of the earliest and most influential voices for allowing people to believe and worship as they choose.

In late 1685, while Locke was living in political exile in Amsterdam, he wrote a long Latin letter to his Dutch friend Philip von Limborch, which was later published anonymously in May 1689 under the title *Epistola de Tolerantia* (*A Letter Concerning Toleration*). Locke was moved by the plight of French Huguenots fleeing persecution in France following the revocation of the Edict of Nantes in October 1685. He was also worried that the new Catholic king of England, James II, might prove intolerant to non-Catholics in England. Locke had seen firsthand how successfully religious toleration worked in Holland; his hope was that England would follow the Dutch example.

In *Epistola* he argues that the "care of souls" is simply not the state's business. The purpose of government is to protect basic rights and freedoms, not to impose religious beliefs. To insist that force may be used to coerce religious conformity is to sow a pernicious "seed of discord and war." Moreover, "only light and evidence ... can work a change in men's opinions"; coercion produces hypocrites and martyrs, not sincere believers. Finally, the Gospels and apostles teach that "no man can be a Christian without charity, and without that faith which works, not by force, but by love."

Locke was not an advocate of complete religious freedom. He argued that governments should not tolerate religions that cause concrete harms or seek to undermine the foundations of society. Nor should they tolerate atheists (who lack the moral backbone to be reliable citizens) or Roman Catholics (who profess allegiance to a foreign power, the pope). Here Locke was a step behind the farsighted American Puritan Roger Williams (c. 1603–83), who argued for complete religious liberty, even for "paganish, Jewish, Turkish or anti-Christian consciences and worships," in his remarkable *Bloudy Tenent of Persecution* (1644).

> In Epistola [Locke] argues that the . . . purpose of government is to protect basic rights and freedoms, not to impose religious beliefs.

SEE ALSO Human Rights (1689)

EMPIRICISM

John Locke (1632–1704)

IN LOCKE'S DAY, most philosophers believed that some ideas are innate—that is, present in the mind (at least implicitly or inchoately) from birth. Popular candidates for inborn ideas included the idea of God, basic moral concepts, and fundamental logical principles like "no proposition can be both true and false." Locke argued that there are no innate ideas or principles. All ideas come from experience—chiefly sense experience. Locke's forceful and influential arguments for this view made him "the father of modern empiricism."

In *An Essay Concerning Human Understanding* (1689), Locke maintains that if innate ideas exist, then literally everybody would have them. But there is no reason to think that infants, for example, have an idea of God or a knowledge of right and wrong. If it is retorted that such ideas are "virtually" or "seminally" innate in babies' minds, this is either trivially true or nonsensical. It is trivially true if what is meant is that babies are capable of forming such ideas when they get older. No one denies that. And it is nonsensical if what is meant is that babies have such ideas but are not yet able to consciously access them. It makes no sense,

As an empiricist, Locke believed that all ideas come either from the senses or through introspection on our own thoughts and feelings.

Locke argues, to say you "have" an idea that is totally unconscious and unavailable.

As an empiricist, Locke believed that all ideas come either from the senses or through introspection on our own thoughts and feelings—what he calls "ideas of reflection." Locke also argues that we have no direct knowledge of the world as it exists outside our heads; all we ever know directly are our own ideas and sensations. In other words, all awareness of the world is mediated awareness; all we know directly is how the world *appears* to us. This raises an obvious opening for skepticism. How do we know that we are not dreaming or that that which we call "life" is not some huge hoax perpetrated by a mind-controlling demon or evil extraterrestrial scientists? Locke dismisses such doubts as mere academic pettifogging. But other empiricists, like Berkeley and Hume in the eighteenth century, would take them much more seriously.

SEE ALSO To Be Is to Be Perceived (1713), *A Treatise of Human Nature* (1739), *Pragmatism* (1907)

TO BE IS TO BE PERCEIVED

George Berkeley (1685–1753)

All that exists, according to George Berkeley, are spirits
(God, human souls, and angels) and their ideas. Here, God the Father
holds court among a choir of angels in a detail from an engraving by
Flemish artists Maerten de Vos and Jan Collaert II, c. 1590.

THERE WERE THREE GREAT BRITISH EMPIRICISTS in early modern philosophy: John Locke, who was English; George Berkeley, who was Irish (of English descent); and David Hume (1711–76), who was Scottish. Locke and Hume are mostly on the same page, though Hume takes empiricism in a much more skeptical direction than Locke does. Berkeley is in many ways the odd man out. He was an Anglican bishop and a staunch defender of Christian orthodoxy against atheists, skeptics, and freethinkers. Yet he argued for the seemingly irrational view that matter does not exist. All that exists, Berkeley contends, are spirits (God, human souls, and angels) and their ideas. For so-called physical objects, such as rocks and stars and trees, his theory was *esse is percipi* (to be is to be perceived). This is a view called "Idealism" or "Immaterialism." Berkeley's greatness as a philosopher lies in how ingeniously he argues for this seemingly paradoxical view. It helped that he was also perhaps the greatest writer of English philosophical prose who ever lived.

Berkeley was born near Kilkenny, Ireland. After graduating from Trinity College, Dublin, he became a fellow there in 1707. All of his most important philosophical work was written before he was thirty years old. His greatest work, *A Treatise Concerning the Principles of Human Knowledge*, was published in 1710. Disappointed by its reception, Berkeley published a more popular version of his idealist theory in *Three Dialogues between Hylas and Philonous* in 1713. From 1728 to 1732, Berkeley waited in vain in Newport, Rhode Island, for funds from the British government to found a college in Bermuda. In 1734, he was appointed bishop of Cloyne, in southern Ireland, where he served until he retired to Oxford in 1752.

Berkeley offered a battery of arguments to try to show that the concept of matter was unintelligible, unneeded, and dangerous to religion. Some of the arguments he advanced against the idea of material substance applied just as well to the notion of spiritual substance. It was left to the next great empiricist, David Hume, to throw out the concept of substance altogether.

SEE ALSO Empiricism (1689), *A Treatise of Human Nature* (1739)

THE MORAL SENSE

Anthony Ashley-Cooper,
3rd Earl of Shaftesbury (Lord Shaftesbury) (1671–1713),
Francis Hutcheson (1694–1746)

MOST PEOPLE WOULD SAY they *know* certain moral truths, such as that cruelty to animals is wrong. But *how* do we know such things? What "faculty" or mental processes do we use in making such judgments? Prior to about 1700, the conventional answer among Western philosophers was that we use *reason*. We obtain moral knowledge by using the same methods of reasoning and intuition that we use in math or science, a view known as "moral rationalism."

In the eighteenth century, moral rationalism came under attack from a group of British thinkers known today as "moral-sense theorists" or "moral sentimentalists." The four most important moral-sense theorists were Lord Shaftesbury, Francis Hutcheson, David Hume, and Adam Smith (1723–90). Shaftesbury sketched a version of moral-sense theory in *Characteristics of Men, Manners, Opinions, Times* (1711), but the first systematic presentation of the theory was offered by Hutcheson in *An Inquiry into the Original of Our Ideas of Beauty and Virtue* (1725).

Shaftesbury and Hutcheson were struck by the fact that often our moral reactions are immediate and involuntary. For example, if we see someone mistreating a child, we instantly get upset and have strong feelings of moral disapproval. Yet reason operates too slowly to explain these reactions. Moreover, if all our ideas come from experience, as Locke was thought to have shown, where do we get our ideas of moral goodness and badness? Presumably from the senses. But not from our five ordinary senses, which only reveal physical properties of things. So our ideas of moral goodness and badness must come from a special faculty of sensation, the moral sense.

God, they believed, has endowed us with a conscience, or moral sense, that perceives moral beauty and ugliness, much as our aesthetic sense perceives artistic beauty or ugliness. Reason may come into play later to verify or to systematize the intimations of moral sense, but moral sense is primary.

Shaftesbury and Hutcheson's moral-sense theory provoked a huge century-long debate in British philosophy between defenders of moral rationalism, such as Joseph Butler (1692–1752), John Balguy (1686–1748), and Richard Price (1723–91), and the new upstart moral sentimentalists. In some ways, the debate continues today.

> Our ideas of moral goodness and badness must come from a special faculty of sensation, the moral sense.

SEE ALSO Natural Law (c. 1270), Empiricism (1689), Morality Is Rooted in Feeling (1751), Ethical Intuitionism (1903)

DEISM

Matthew Tindal (1657–1733)

THERE ARE TWO VIEWS that commonly go by the name of "deism." One is the idea of an absentee or clockmaker God who made the world, gave it its laws, and then left it to run on its own. The other is the view that true religion is "natural religion," that is, truths about God can be learned solely by means of reason and the observation of nature, without resort to any alleged divine revelation. This latter form of deism was defended by a number of important seventeenth- and eighteenth-century thinkers, including John Toland (1670–1722), Anthony Collins (1676–1729), Voltaire (1694–1778), and Thomas Paine (1737–1809). Philosophically, the most important defense of deism was Matthew Tindal's 1730 book, *Christianity as Old as the Creation*.

An Oxford don and lawyer, Tindal argued that an all-wise and all-good God would not have revealed his will and essential truths of religion to only a small percentage of mankind. The Bible, therefore, is not the word of God. The core truths of religion can be discerned by the pure light of reason alone. Those core truths are simply that an infinitely perfect Creator exists, that God wishes us to be happy, and that we serve God best by trying to do as much good as we can. This simple creed is what true Christianity is all about. Such a creed has been evident throughout human history. Accordingly, Christianity is "as old as the creation."

Tindal's book created a firestorm. Within a few years, over 150 replies were published, including William Law's *The Case of Reason* (1731), George Berkeley's *Alciphron* (1732), and Joseph Butler's *The Analogy of Religion* (1736).

A number of America's founding fathers were deists, including Benjamin Franklin and Thomas Jefferson. Franklin stated that he believed in "one

Supreme most perfect being," but doubted that such a being "does in the least regard such an inconsiderable nothing as man." Jefferson advised his nephew to "fix reason firmly in her seat, and call to her tribunal every fact, every opinion. Question with boldness even the existence of a God; because, if there be one, he must more approve the homage of reason than of blindfolded fear."

Tindal argued that . . . the core truths of religion can be discerned by the pure light of reason alone.

SEE ALSO Hume's *Dialogues* (1779)

A TREATISE OF HUMAN NATURE

David Hume (1711–76)

DAVID HUME IS WIDELY CONSIDERED to be the greatest of all British philosophers. He was born in Edinburgh, Scotland, and educated at the University of Edinburgh. His first book, *A Treatise of Human Nature*, made little splash when it was first published, though it is now generally considered to be his masterwork. Other than the Treatise, Hume's three most important philosophical works are *An Enquiry Concerning Human Understanding* (1748), *An Enquiry Concerning the Principles of Morals* (1751), and the *Dialogues Concerning Natural Religion* (1779).

In his momentous early work *A Treatise of Human Nature* (1739–40), Hume sought to apply the "experimental method" of investigation that had proved so successful in the natural sciences to the study of human subjects. In the process, Hume showed how empiricism leads ineluctably to various forms of skepticism. If all human ideas derive from experience, then any apparent idea that cannot be traced back to experience must be a pseudo-idea. This is a notion that later philosophers have dubbed "the empirical criterion of meaning." According to this test, all genuine or meaningful ideas can in principle be traced to some original sensory or introspective impression. Hume wields this empirical criterion of meaning like a sword to cut through huge swaths of traditional philosophy, including ideas of causation, the self, objective morality, and an independently existing external world.

Consider causation. The ordinary notion of causation supposes that some events cause other events by means of some kind of causal "power" or "necessary connection." But do we ever actually experience causal power or necessity? No, Hume argues; all we ever perceive are regular sequences of events: A is always followed by B. For all we know, A and B might be totally unrelated events that are part of a story that some mind controller has planted in our heads. Thus, Hume argued, the traditional idea of causation is empirically unwarranted. The only meaningful idea of causation we have is that of "constant conjunction": A, in our experience, has always been followed by B, and we have a strong psychological propensity to believe that this pattern will continue in the future.

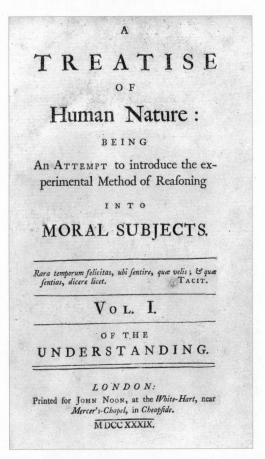

A

TREATISE

OF

Human Nature :

BEING

An ATTEMPT to introduce the experimental Method of Reasoning

INTO

MORAL SUBJECTS.

Rara temporum felicitas, ubi sentire, quæ velis ; & quæ sentias, dicere licet.   TACIT.

VOL. I.

OF THE

UNDERSTANDING.

LONDON:
Printed for JOHN NOON, at the *White-Hart,* near *Mercer's-Chapel,* in *Cheapside.*
MDCCXXXIX.

The title page from *Of the Understanding,* volume I of Hume's *A Treatise of Human Nature,* 1739, published in London.

SEE ALSO The Problem of Induction (1739), Morality Is Rooted in Feeling (1751), Logical Positivism (1936)

THE PROBLEM OF INDUCTION

David Hume (1711–76)

Steel engraving of David Hume, 1843.

ONE OF THE MANY POWERFUL skeptical challenges offered in Hume's *Treatise of Human Nature* (1739–40) is what is now called the "problem of induction." The problem centrally involves reasoning that tries to predict the future based on things we have observed in the past. Hume's stunning conclusion is that no such predictions can be rationally justified.

Hume's account of the problem of induction is a bit complex, so let me briefly sketch the problem in more contemporary terms. Consider our belief that the law of gravity will continue to operate tomorrow. What evidence do we have for this? Well, in the past the law of gravity has always held true, so is it not reasonable to suppose it will continue to operate tomorrow? But here Hume noticed something very interesting. Why is the past any guide to the future at all? If nature were totally anarchic and the laws of nature changed every half-second, the past would not be a reliable guide to the future. So whenever we make predictions we are assuming that nature is substantially uniform, that the future will (substantially) resemble the past. Call this assumption "the principle of uniformity."

Now Hume asks, what evidence do we have that the principle of uniformity is true? Because it has held true in the past? But then we are assuming that the past is a reliable guide to the future, which means we are using the principle of uniformity to try to prove the principle of uniformity, which is reasoning in a circle. It seems, in fact, that there is no noncircular way of arguing for the principle of uniformity at all. Not a single bit of real evidence can be produced that it is true. Yet the principle of uniformity is not self-evident; we can easily imagine it turning out to be false. Hume's conclusion is that all inductive (that is, probabilistic) inferences that try to predict the future are based on what he calls "instinct" or "custom," not reason. Nature has just hardwired us, as it has many animals, to expect the future to go on much like the past. As Hume sees it, reason plays a much less significant role in human existence than most philosophers have thought.

SEE ALSO *A Treatise of Human Nature* (1739)

AN ATTACK ON MIRACLES

David Hume (1711–76)

Hundreds of people, including a woman named Margueritte Françoise du Chêne—
depicted in the center of this eighteenth-century engraving—were said to be
miraculously cured in 1731 at the tomb of François de Pâris (1690–1727), an
ascetic French Catholic deacon, in the cemetery of St. Médard, Paris.

IN SECTION X of *An Enquiry Concerning Human Understanding* (1748), Hume offers a famous argument against miracles. He does not argue that miracles are impossible, a claim that would be at odds with his empiricist starting points. His contention, rather, is that it is never reasonable to believe that a miracle has occurred, no matter how strongly it may appear to be supported by human testimony. His argument has two parts: First he gives a general argument why the burden of proof is extremely high in cases of alleged miracles. Then he offers some specific reasons for thinking that this burden of proof has never, in fact, come close to having been met.

The specific reasons Hume mentions are mostly conventional worries about the credibility of miracle stories (for example, the fact that they "are observed chiefly to abound among ignorant and barbarous nations"). Of greater interest and originality is the preliminary argument Hume gives for why we should be highly suspicious of miracle stories in general. A miracle, Hume says, is a violation of a law of nature. Nothing is called a law of nature unless it is supported by abundant and absolutely uniform evidence. Such evidence, Hume argues, amounts to a certainty, or what he calls a "proof," that such laws will continue to operate without exceptions. Whenever we hear or read about an alleged miracle, we must balance this proof against the likelihood that the witness is either lying or mistaken. At best, Hume argues, any human testimony for a miracle can amount only to a "probability," not to a proof. A wise man proportions his belief to the evidence. Proofs provide stronger evidence than do probabilities. So a wise man will always disbelieve testimony for a miracle unless the falsehood of the report would be even more miraculous than the alleged miracle itself. Such a high burden of proof, Hume argues, has never remotely been met. With every actual miracle report, it is always much more likely that the testifier is lying or mistaken than that a law of nature has been broken.

SEE ALSO *A Treatise of Human Nature* (1739), The Problem of Induction (1739)

MORALITY IS ROOTED IN FEELING

David Hume (1711–76)

AS WE HAVE SEEN, there was a long-running debate in eighteenth-century Britain between moral rationalists, who believed that ethics is based in reason, and moral sentimentalists, who believed that ethics is rooted in feeling. In 1751, David Hume published *An Enquiry Concerning the Principles of Morals*. There, Hume offered powerful support for the sentimentalist view.

> Hume identifies two natural human feelings that he believed lay at the root of ethics: benevolence and sympathy.

Like Francis Hutcheson, to whom Hume was heavily indebted in ethics, Hume was struck by the similarity between judgments of beauty and judgments of morality. Hume believed that Hutcheson had convincingly demonstrated that aesthetic and moral qualities are subjective, or perceiver dependent, in the same way that sounds, tastes, and colors are. As a strict empiricist, Hume held that there was no viable basis for belief in objective moral properties. Our senses cannot perceive objective moral properties, nor can our reason, which Hume claimed deals only with "relations of ideas" (like math and logic) and "matters of fact" (that is, factual beliefs that are based on sense impressions). As Hutcheson claimed, morality is rooted in human nature—specifically in feeling or sentiment. Hume identifies two natural human feelings that he believed lay at the root of ethics: benevolence and sympathy. Humans naturally approve of acts of kindness and beneficence, and feel distress when observing others in pain. What we call "virtues" are qualities like justice, honesty, and cheerfulness that are "either useful or agreeable to the person himself or to others." This makes morality subjective in the sense that moral judgments depend on feeling rather than on rational insight or perception of mind-independent moral qualities. But morality is also objective inasmuch as it is rooted in more or less universal human feelings and instincts.

One striking conclusion that follows from Hume's view is a complete reversal of the traditional conception of the relationship between reason and emotion. Since Plato, Western philosophers had generally agreed that emotion must be subordinate to reason. Hume inverted this, claiming that "reason is, and ought only to be, the slave of the passions." And this is true not only in ethics. As Hume saw it, pretty much the entire structure of human belief is rooted in feeling and instinct.

SEE ALSO The Moral Sense (1725), *A Treatise of Human Nature* (1739)

CANDIDE

François-Marie Arouet (Voltaire) (1694–1778)

IN TRYING TO MAKE SENSE of our world from a religious perspective, many philosophers have taught either that there are no genuine evils (because what appears to be evil is actually good) or that there are no "pointless" or "gratuitous" evils, that is, evils that do not result in greater goods. This latter idea was encapsulated in a famous slogan by the German mathematician and philosopher Gottfried Wilhem Leibniz (1646–1716) that God has created "the best of all possible worlds." In *Candide, ou l'optimisme* (1759), the French writer and philosopher Voltaire satirizes this kind of baseless optimism in one of the great short stories of all time.

Voltaire (the pen name of François-Marie Arouet) was a controversial figure during his lifetime and remains so today. As a writer, he was loved for his wit, vitality, and sparkling storytelling skills. Yet his unrelenting attacks on organized religion, autocratic government, war, religious intolerance, and an inhumane criminal justice system made him many enemies.

Candide is a madcap tale of the incredible misadventures of a young man named Candide; his eternally optimistic tutor, Professor Pangloss; Candide's love-interest, Cunégonde; and Candide's faithful servant, Cacambo, as they travel the world meeting with one tragic misfortune after another. No matter what calamity strikes them, Professor Pangloss sticks to his Leibnizian optimism, always managing to find some redeeming good in every personal tragedy. By the end of the book, however, Candide's eyes have been opened; his final enigmatic advice in this world of follies and woe is to "cultivate our garden."

Philosophically, the most interesting question *Candide* raises is whether theism implies that this is the best of all possible worlds. Leibniz argues that it does, claiming that an all-powerful, all-wise, and all-good God would survey all the possible universes he could create and actualize that one that has the best overall balance of good over evil. In advancing his argument, Leibniz assumes first that there is some maximally good world, and secondly that a perfectly good God would follow a utilitarian strategy of maximizing net happiness. Both of these assumptions can be questioned. Thus, contrary to Leibniz, there may be ways of reconciling belief in a perfect God with the existence of an obviously imperfect world.

Philosophically, the most interesting question *Candide* raises is whether theism implies that this is the best of all possible worlds.

SEE ALSO Soul-Making Theodicy (1966)

THE BIRTH OF ROMANTICISM

Jean-Jacques Rousseau (1712–78)

ROMANTICISM WAS A COMPLEX and multifaceted cultural movement in Western history that extended from roughly the 1760s to the late 1850s. Broadly, it was a revolt against Enlightenment rationalism. Romantics exalted feeling over reason, art over science, nature over civilization, solitude over society, mysticism over organized religion, and individual freedom over social order. The Romantic movement had a profound impact on literature, art, architecture, music, education, politics, environmentalism, theology, and philosophy. Though its beginnings were complex, one important early influence was Jean-Jacques Rousseau, particularly his sentimentalist novel *Julie, or the New Heloise* (1761), his novelistic educational treatise *Emile* (1762), and, above all, his shockingly outspoken autobiography, *The Confessions* (1782). Throughout these works, Rousseau pounds home the notion that feelings are a better guide to truth than reason is.

Rousseau's ideas on democracy, popular sovereignty, and equality strongly influenced the politics of the French Revolution. In Germany, Immanuel Kant stressed the limits of human reason and grounded religion in moral feeling, and Arthur Schopenhauer's exaltation of the will and of art breathed the very spirit of Romanticism. In America, the transcendentalist movement of Ralph Waldo Emerson and Henry David Thoreau reflected clearly the individualistic, mystical, and nature-centered themes of the Age of Feeling. The influences of Romanticism are reflected in the Rousseauian educational thought of J. H. Pestalozzi and Friedrich Fröbel, Samuel Taylor Coleridge's distinction between spirit-attuned Reason and spirit-blind Understanding, and the nature-mysticism of John Muir.

The decline of Romanticism can be dated roughly to the publication of Charles Darwin's *On the Origin of Species* in 1859. Romanticism was at bottom a revolt against the horrors of the Industrial Revolution and the cold, mechanistic world that science seemed to have revealed. As economic conditions improved in the latter half of the nineteenth century and the prestige of science grew, philosophers in both Europe and America increasingly returned to Enlightenment ideals of reason, science, and optimism, though the impact of Romanticism continued to be felt.

An engraving after the noted portrait of Rousseau painted by Scottish artist Allan Ramsay in 1766 when Rousseau came to Britain.

SEE ALSO The Enlightenment Begins (1620), *Emile* and Natural Education (1762)

THE SOCIAL CONTRACT

Jean-Jacques Rousseau (1712–78)

ROUSSEAU HAD A PROFOUND IMPACT not only on philosophy, but also on politics, literature, art, education, and manners. His influence on Romanticism and education will be considered in other entries. Here we look at his political thought, particularly as expressed in *The Social Contract*, his most important book.

Rousseau, who led a turbulent and troubled life, was born in Geneva, Switzerland, in 1712, the son of a poor watchmaker. After his father abandoned the family around 1724, Rousseau largely raised and educated himself. His first book, *Discourse on the Arts and Sciences* (1750), shocked French Enlightenment thinkers such as Diderot and Voltaire by attacking civilization, science, and reason. His next major work, *Discourse on the Origins of Inequality* (1755), argued that humans are naturally good; painted an idyllic picture of a primitive, pre-social state of nature; and blamed private property as the origin of oppressive inequalities. *In The Social Contract* (1762), Rousseau made clear that he wasn't attacking government and social order per se. On the contrary, he argued, only through organized communities can humans truly be ethical and free.

> Fostering the communal good, [Rousseau] says, is also our own "real will," what all of us explicitly or implicitly desire.

The problem Rousseau wrestles with in *The Social Contract* is how to reconcile government and freedom. When humans decide to leave the state of nature by creating governments and laws, they surrender their "natural liberty" to do as they please, unhindered by laws or other people. But in creating governments they acquire a higher type of freedom that Rousseau calls "civil liberty." True liberty, he argues, is living under laws that we ourselves have made. When humans elect to leave the state of nature and form a community, they create an artificial person, a sovereign body, with a will of its own—"the general will"—which is basically the collective desire to promote the common good. Fostering the communal good, he says, is also our own "real will," what all of us explicitly or implicitly desire. Therefore there is no real sacrifice of freedom when we obey laws, even those with which we may strongly disagree. In fact, lawbreakers may be "forced to be free" by state coercion, a notion that many contemporary philosophers regard as paradoxical and fraught with peril.

SEE ALSO *Leviathan* (1651), Human Rights (1689), The Birth of Romanticism (c. 1760)

EMILE AND NATURAL EDUCATION

Jean-Jacques Rousseau (1712–78)

An illustration from an eighteenth-century edition
of Rousseau's *Emile, or on Education.*

ROUSSEAU IS THE FOUNTAINHEAD of many important developments in the modern world, including what we today call child-centered education. His vision of education is laid out in his charming book *Emile, or on Education* (1762). Like everything Rousseau wrote, it is full of exaggerations and absurdities, but it remains a seminal work of educational theory.

Emile is the story, written in novelistic form, of a rich young boy (Emile) and his dedicated tutor, who devotes over twenty years to Emile's private education. Rousseau believed that humans are naturally good and that civilization corrupts. As he saw it, the proper task of education is thus to preserve and develop a child's natural goodness to the greatest degree possible. To do this, Emile's tutor raises him in the country, far from the vicious influences of the city. Emile's education is divided into three stages: childhood (ages 0–12), youth (ages 13–20), and young adulthood (21 until roughly 25). The first stage is completely nonintellectual. Its goal is to preserve the heart from vice and the mind from error by keeping the mental faculties inactive until they have matured. The motto at this stage is "Let childhood ripen in children." What learning takes place occurs mostly through outdoor play, active doing, feeling, and firsthand experience, not through books or verbal lessons.

Emile's formal education begins in early adolescence. At this time he is introduced to books, but mostly he learns by doing and experience. He also learns a useful trade so that he can earn a living if necessary. He knows nothing at this stage about history, philosophy, or religion. When Emile is taught religion, it is only a simple theistic creed; he is left to choose whether he wishes to follow any particular sect. It is only in the young-adult period of education that Emile studies history and develops his own sense of taste, mingles in society, travels, and actively prepares for married life. The last book of *Emile* is devoted to the largely domestic education of Emile's ideal mate, Sophie. According to Rousseau, a woman's essential role in life is to be a sweet, useful, and agreeable stay-at-home helpmate.

SEE ALSO Progressive Education (1916)

A GODLESS, MECHANISTIC UNIVERSE

Paul-Henri Thiry, Baron d'Holbach (1723–89)

IN THE MIDDLE OF THE EIGHTEENTH CENTURY, a group of like-minded public intellectuals called the "philosophes" popularized Enlightenment ideals in France. Many of these thinkers were associated with the famous *Encyclopédie* (1751–72) edited by Denis Diderot (1713–84) and Jean le Rond d'Alembert (1717–83). The philosophes were opposed to the established political order and to organized religion, particularly the Catholic Church. Though some of the philosophes were deists, others were agnostics or atheists. The most outspoken atheist was Paul-Henri Thiry, Baron d'Holbach.

Holbach was born in Germany, the son of a vintner, but he was raised in Paris by his uncle, a rich stock speculator and French nobleman. After graduating from the University of Leiden in Holland, Holbach married and began contributing numerous articles to the *Encyclopédie*. In 1753, Holbach inherited his uncle's title and estate, making him wealthy for life. The following year, Holbach's wife died. He later married his wife's younger sister. In 1761, Holbach published *Christianity Unveiled*, an attack on Christianity and its moral influences. Thereafter, Holbach poured out a constant stream of antireligious books, including his most important work, *The System of Nature* (1770), referred to as "the Bible of atheism" by his opponents. All of his books were published anonymously or under false names.

Holbach was a materialist who believed that nothing exists except matter in motion. He was also a strict determinist, claiming everything that occurs in nature is necessitated by prior events and that free will is an illusion. Any fully satisfactory explanation of events, he claimed, must be mechanistic, referring only to matter, motion, and the laws that govern the movement of material particles.

Holbach used his great wealth to host fabulous parties at his townhouse in Paris and his country estate at Grandval in southern France. Many leading philosophes and distinguished guests met at Holbach's salon. Among Holbach's famous guests was David Hume. The first time Hume dined with Holbach, he remarked that he had never met a real atheist. Holbach responded that of the eighteen other guests at the table, fifteen were avowed atheists and three had not yet made up their minds.

> [Holbach] believed that nothing exists except matter in motion. . . . Any fully satisfactory explanation of events, he claimed, must be mechanistic.

SEE ALSO Atoms and the Void (c. 420 BCE), The Enlightenment Begins (1620), The New Atheists (2004)

HUME'S *DIALOGUES*

David Hume (1711–76)

IN THE EIGHTEENTH CENTURY it was widely believed that the wonderful order, complexity, and beauty of the world provides clear evidence of the existence of God. This so-called argument from design was powerfully challenged in David Hume's posthumously published *Dialogues Concerning Natural Religion* (1779).

There are three participants in the *Dialogues*: Demea, an orthodox Christian who tries to prove God's existence as the first cause of the universe; Cleanthes, a deist who defends the argument from design; and Philo, a skeptic, who denies that God's existence can be proved. Most scholars believe that it is Philo who speaks most directly for Hume.

Hume offers a barrage of arguments against the argument from design. How can we reconcile the idea of an all-benevolent God with all the pain and suffering we see in the world? How can we infer the existence of an all-perfect God from a far-from-perfect world? If order and complexity imply intelligent design, what explains the order and complexity of ideas in God's mind? Finally, how strong is the analogy between human-made machines and a God-made world-machine? Machines are usually built by many workers. Why suppose that only a single god made the world? How do we know that the world is not "the production of old age and dotage in some superannuated Deity" who has long since expired, or "the first rude essay of some infant deity, who afterwards abandoned it"? Why should not many universes "have been botched and bungled, throughout an eternity, ere this system was struck out"? At best, Hume argues, the argument from design shows that "the cause or causes of order in the universe probably bear some remote analogy to human intelligence." Beyond this vague and tentative supposition, not a single step can be taken.

Despite Hume's powerful attack, the argument from design continued to attract influential defenders. Less than a quarter-century after Hume's *Dialogues* appeared, English cleric and philosopher William Paley (1743–1805) published his famous work, *Natural Theology* (1802), which offered an elaborate defense of the argument. It was Darwin, not Hume, however, who delivered the most serious blow to the argument from design.

Hume wondered how strong the analogy is between human-made machines, such as the steam engine invented by British engineer Thomas Newcomen in 1712—shown here in a nineteenth-century illustration—and a God-made world-machine.

SEE ALSO The Five Ways (c. 1265), Deism (1730)

CRITIQUE OF PURE REASON

Immanuel Kant (1724–1804)

IMMANUEL KANT'S *Critique of Pure Reason* was a huge watershed in philosophy. The book's central idea—that the world as we experience it is mostly a construct of the human mind—dominated nineteenth-century thought and is still accepted by many philosophers today.

Kant's life will never be made into a movie; it was rich in ideas but not in adventures. He was born in Königsberg (then part of East Prussia but now Kaliningrad, in a noncontiguous part of Russia). Aside from a few short trips, Kant lived his entire life in his native city, where he taught at the University of Königsberg for many decades. A late bloomer, Kant published all of his major philosophical works after the age of fifty-six. His most important books are the *Critique of Pure Reason* (1781), *Groundwork of the Metaphysics of Morals* (1785), *Critique of Practical Reason* (1788), and *Critique of Judgment* (1790). Like many great philosophers, he never married.

Kant was troubled by both Hume's corrosive skepticism and the failure of traditional metaphysics to provide a secure foundation for belief in God, objective morality, free will, and life after death. Unlike Hume, Kant believed that we know necessary truths about empirical and moral reality (for example, we know that every event must have a cause). As Hume had argued, it is impossible for us to acquire such knowledge through experience. Kant's solution was to say that the human mind has certain innate, built-in structures that automatically process all possible experiences into certain predetermined forms. The mind, as it were, has certain hardwired cookie-cutter patterns that it imposes on all possible experiences. The upshot is that we can never know reality as it is itself (what Kant calls "noumenal reality"); we can only know "phenomenal reality," reality as it appears to us. Ultimately, Kant argues, reason cannot prove that God exists or that we have free will or that there will be an afterlife. However, our moral experience makes no sense without these underpinning beliefs, so they can be supported by a kind of rational faith.

OPPOSITE: An engraving of Immanuel Kant published in the German encyclopedia *Meyers Konversations-Lexikon*, 1859.

SEE ALSO *A Treatise of Human Nature* (1739), The Problem of Induction (1739)

1785

THE CATEGORICAL IMPERATIVE

Immanuel Kant (1724–1804)

KANT IS AN IMPORTANT ETHICIST for a number of reasons. First, he is the founding father of deontological, or duty-centered, ethics, which has been a leading moral theory for over two centuries. Second, he is a major influence on modern ethical theories that emphasize the inherent dignity or worth of all human beings. Finally, he formulated a basic moral principle, the so-called categorical imperative, which has generated a great deal of interest and discussion.

> Kant's general drift is clear enough: It is wrong to do something that you would not want others to do in your exact situation.

Kant was raised in a pious Protestant family, and he believed that the Golden Rule of Jesus—do unto others as you would have others do unto you—captured something at the heart of morality. But Kant noted that the Golden Rule has certain limitations. For instance, it says nothing about duties to self, such as the obligations not to waste one's talents and not to commit suicide. So Kant reformulated the Golden Rule in a way that made it more general and (he believed) more precise. He called this reformulation the categorical imperative to emphasize both that it is a *law* ("imperative" is another word for "command") and that it *binds unconditionally*. Confusingly, Kant offers four different formulations of the categorical imperative. The first and most famous version is this: "I should never act in such a way that I could not also will that my maxim should be a universal law."

It is uncertain how exactly this should be interpreted. Kant is not very clear what he means by a "maxim" or how we should go about formulating the maxims that implicitly underlie our contemplated actions. But Kant's general drift is clear enough: It is wrong to do something that you would not want others to do in your exact situation. Put otherwise, it is unethical to treat yourself as a "special case," exempt from moral rules that you yourself admit are reasonable and just. There are difficulties when you apply Kant's categorical imperative to certain cases. In particular, it is not clear that Kant's principle will rule out all immoral acts or produce the kinds of universally applicable moral standards Kant seeks. But the core insight expressed by the categorical imperative has great intuitive appeal.

SEE ALSO Reciprocity (c. 500 BCE), Deontological Intuitionism (1930)

1787

THE FEDERALIST

Alexander Hamilton (1755/57–1804),
James Madison (1751–1836), John Jay (1745–1829)

THOMAS JEFFERSON—no slouch as a political thinker—described *The Federalist* in 1787 as "the best commentary on the principles of government which ever was written." Together with the Declaration of Independence, the US Constitution, the Bill of Rights, and the Gettysburg Address, it remains one of the foundational documents of American government. *The Federalist* (or *Federalist Papers*) consists of eighty-five essays, most of which were published in New York City newspapers between October 1787 and April 1788. The purpose was to build support for the ratification of the new Constitution that had been proposed by the Philadelphia Convention in September 1787. New York County assemblyman Alexander Hamilton— soon to be the first secretary of the treasury—proposed the project and wrote the lion's share of the articles. Virginia delegate and future US president James Madison contributed about thirty essays, including some of the most brilliant. New York lawyer John Jay, who later became the nation's first chief justice, wrote five.

The Federalist is a masterpiece of political debate. Its combination of learning, eloquence, and powerful compact reasoning overwhelmed the Constitution's numerous opponents and helped secure ratification in closely fought states like New York and Virginia. As a contribution to political philosophy, *The Federalist* is most important for its sustained case for a new vision of republican government. At the time, it was widely believed that any large state would inevitably become unjust and undemocratic. The *Federalist* authors successfully rebutted this assumption by arguing that the proposed Constitution's elaborate safeguards—including checks and balances, separation of powers, and staggered and indirect elections—allowed

A nineteenth-century engraving of James Madison; Madison's *Federalist* No. 10, "The Utility of the Union as a Safeguard Against Domestic Faction and Insurrection" (November 22, 1787), is considered the seminal *Federalist* essay.

for an energetic national government that wouldn't trample on people's rights. Moreover, as Madison famously argued in *Federalist* No. 10, the great diversity of American life would make it difficult for oppressive "factions" to unite to cause mischief at the federal level. Today, we recognize that some of *The Federalist*'s predictions were overly rosy, and that the original Constitution was not perfect. But Americans continue to feel great pride in what is the oldest written charter of government in the world. A good deal of credit for that is due to *The Federalist*.

SEE ALSO Human Rights (1689)

UTILITARIANISM

Jeremy Bentham (1748–1832)

SEVERAL EIGHTEENTH-CENTURY THINKERS, including David Hartley (1705–57) and Francis Hutcheson (1694–1746), defended versions of the principle of utility, also called the greatest happiness principle. According to this principle, an act is morally right if and only if it produces "the greatest happiness of the greatest number," or, more precisely, brings about more net happiness than any alternative action could have produced. The thinker who first popularized the principle of utility was the English philosopher and political reformer Jeremy Bentham.

Bentham was a brilliant but odd man. Born in London, he was a precocious child, graduating from the University of Oxford at the age of fifteen. After obtaining a law degree, Bentham was appalled by the inhumane and incoherent condition of English law and decided to devote his life to legal and political reform. He became the leader of a group of reformers known as the Philosophical Radicals, or Benthamites, cofounded a journal (the *Westminster Review*), and wrote tirelessly. For some strange reason, he left many of his works unfinished and only published a tiny proportion of what he wrote. Probably the most important work he did publish is *An Introduction to the Principles of Morals and Legislation* (1789). There he explains and defends the principle of utility and works out a system of ethics and law based on that principle.

Bentham was a systematizer. He loved to work out elaborate classifications in which everything was fleshed out properly and had its logical cubbyhole. One example of this is his so-called hedonic, or felicific, calculus. This is a method for figuring out which act, of all those one could perform, is likely to produce the greatest amount of pleasure. There are seven factors that must be considered: the intensity of the pleasure, its duration, its certainty, its propinquity (how soon the pleasure will occur), its fecundity (how likely it is to produce other pleasures), its purity (whether it is entirely pleasurable or mixed with some pain), and its extent (how many people are affected by it). By means of this calculus, Bentham hoped to make a kind of science of pleasure. And certainly if pleasure is your goal, these are the sorts of factors you should consider.

> Bentham was a systematizer. . . . [He] hoped to make a kind of science of pleasure.

SEE ALSO Cyrenaic Hedonism (c. 400 BCE), Epicureanism (c. 300 BCE), Refined Utilitarianism (1863)

A VINDICATION OF
THE RIGHTS OF WOMAN

Mary Wollstonecraft (1759–97)

MARY WOLLSTONECRAFT'S REPUTATION long suffered from the shocking memoir her husband, William Godwin, published a year after her death. Godwin's indiscreet tales of her illicit affairs, a child born out of wedlock, and two suicide attempts made her a scandalous figure whom few were

An engraving of Mary Wollstonecraft engraved for the *Monthly Mirror*,
a British literary periodical, in 1796.

willing to take seriously. Today, however, she is regarded as an important political thinker and a pioneering advocate of women's rights.

Wollstonecraft led a tumultuous and often unhappy life. Born in London to an abusive and irresponsible father, Wollstonecraft left home early to support herself as a lady's companion, governess, and schoolteacher. Entirely self-educated, Wollstonecraft taught herself French and German and was determined to make a living as a writer. In 1790, she published *A Vindication of the Rights of Men*, a reply to Edmund Burke's *Reflections on the Revolution in France* that brought her considerable notice. Two years later she published her most influential work, *A Vindication of the Rights of Woman*. After two unhappy affairs and a multitude of what John Stuart Mill (1806–73) famously called unconventional "experiments in living," Wollstonecraft married William Godwin (1756–1836), the well-known anarchist and author of *Political Justice* (1793). She died shortly after giving birth to a daughter, Mary, Percy Bysshe Shelley's future wife and the author of *Frankenstein*.

Wollstonecraft's radical conclusions in *A Vindication of the Rights of Woman* are grounded in conventional views of God and human nature. Human dignity, which ultimately flows from God, is rooted in our capacities for reason, virtue, and knowledge. These noble capacities are not unique to men; they are *human* potentialities that should be cultivated by all. Yet men have used their power over women to stunt women's capacities for reason and knowledge and to enfeeble their characters by substituting pseudo-virtues (such as complaisance, timidity, and womanly "sensibility") over genuine ones. Liberating women from such false ideals and educating them as equals would improve their usefulness to society, strengthen marriages, enable them to be better parents and educators of their children, and allow them to achieve their God-given potential as rational and moral agents.

SEE ALSO Emergence of Feminist Philosophy (c. 1976)

THE PHILOSOPHY
OF PESSIMISM

Arthur Schopenhauer (1788–1860)

> Schopenhauer, unlike the Eastern thinkers he admired, did not believe in any kind of permanent liberation or nirvana.

THE NINETEENTH CENTURY was generally a period of optimism and belief in progress. But one great philosopher, the German thinker Arthur Schopenhauer, bucked this trend and defended an uncompromising pessimism. Like Buddha, Schopenhauer believed that life is essentially suffering. But Schopenhauer was much more pessimistic than Buddha about a panacea.

Schopenhauer was born in Danzig (now Gdańsk, Poland). His family was wealthy, which allowed him to spend his life as he wished: as an independent scholar and writer. After obtaining a PhD in philosophy from the University of Jena in Germany, Schopenhauer moved to Dresden, where he wrote his masterwork, *The World as Will and Representation* (1819). Like all of his early writings, it was largely ignored. A brilliant writer, he finally achieved literary success as an essayist. Vain, egotistic, and quarrelsome, Schopenhauer never married and lived alone with a succession of pet poodles.

Schopenhauer was a great admirer of Kant. Like Kant, he believed that what we call "the world" is mostly a construct of the human mind. Kant held that true reality (what he called the noumenal world) is forever unknowable by the human mind. Schopenhauer disagreed.

We ourselves have a true or noumenal self, so we can know true reality through introspection of our own inner experiences. True reality is a timeless and spaceless "force" that Schopenhauer calls Will. In the world as we experience it, Will manifests itself as a blind, restless striving and instinct for survival. When we look at the universe honestly, we see that life is full of violence, conflict, and unsatisfied wants. As Buddha noted, the root cause of suffering is desire. Art can provide a temporary respite from suffering. Longer-lasting relief can be obtained by a Hindu-like resignation in which we accept the inevitability of suffering and curb our desires. But Schopenhauer, unlike the Eastern thinkers he admired, did not believe in any kind of permanent liberation or nirvana. As he saw it, Shakespeare's Macbeth got it right: "Life's but a walking shadow, a poor player / That struts and frets his hour upon the stage / And then is heard no more: it is a tale / Told by an idiot, full of sound and fury, / Signifying nothing."

SEE ALSO The Four Noble Truths (c. 525 BCE), *Critique of Pure Reason* (1781)

AMERICAN TRANSCENDENTALISM

Ralph Waldo Emerson (1803–82)

TRANSCENDENTALISM was the most significant American intellectual movement of the second third of the nineteenth century. At its core, transcendentalism was a Romantic revolt against Puritanism and Enlightenment rationalism and a fervent affirmation of individualism, the divinity of man and nature, and direct spiritual communion with God. Prominent transcendentalists of that time included Henry David Thoreau, Bronson Alcott, Theodore Parker, Margaret Fuller, George Ripley, and Orestes Brownson. But the unofficial leader and prophet of the movement was "the sage of Concord," Ralph Waldo Emerson.

Emerson was born in Boston, the son of a leading Unitarian minister. After graduating from Harvard Divinity School, Emerson served as pastor of a Unitarian church before resigning in 1832 due to his doubts about Christianity and organized religion. For the rest of his life, Emerson supported himself by lecturing and writing, becoming one of America's best-known authors. His 1836 long essay, *Nature*, became something of a credo for the transcendentalist movement.

Strongly influenced by English Romantics such as William Wordsworth (1770–1850) and Samuel Taylor Coleridge (1772–1834), Emerson embraced a form of idealism that views nature as a symbol of spirit, recognizes an element of divinity in the human soul, and sees everything as being (in some mysterious way) "part or parcel of God," or what he sometimes calls the One or the Over-soul. Like many Romantics in that period, Emerson was troubled by the skeptical implications of John Locke's empiricist approach to knowledge. If all our ideas about external reality come from the senses, how is religious experience or moral knowledge possible? To provide a basis for faith and spiritual cognition, Emerson relied on

A nineteenth-century engraving of Ralph Waldo Emerson by American artist John Angel James Wilcox.

Coleridge's distinction between Reason and Understanding. Reason is the eye of the spirit, the faculty by which super-sensuous truths are perceived. Understanding is the faculty that measures, classifies, and arranges information provided by the senses. Emerson essentially identifies Reason with God, thereby divinizing man and making direct spiritual communion possible for everyone. This was a heady doctrine which caught the spirit of the age and resonated well with American ideals of individualism, democracy, self-reliance, and optimism.

SEE ALSO The Birth of Romanticism (c. 1760), *Walden* (1854)

EXISTENTIALISM

Søren Kierkegaard (1813–55)

ONE OF THE MOST INTRIGUING PHILOSOPHIES of the twentieth century was existentialism, which reached its heyday in the 1940s and 1950s, particularly in Europe. Existentialism is not a single, unified philosophy but a cluster of related themes and concerns. It arose as a response both to the challenges of being an authentic individual in an increasingly cookie-cutter world and to the aridity and abstractness of much nineteenth- and twentieth-century philosophy. A major forerunner of existentialism was the nineteenth-century Danish philosopher Søren Kierkegaard.

Kierkegaard epitomized the existentially anguished philosopher. His father, Michael, a wealthy wool merchant, was a melancholic and guilt-ridden man, and Søren struggled all his life with similar feelings. In his college days, Kierkegaard was a dandified socialite, and it took him ten years to finally graduate with a theology degree. Shortly before he graduated, Kierkegaard fell in love with fifteen-year-old Regine Olsen. Three years later they became engaged, but Kierkegaard broke off the engagement in the belief that God had called him to take a different, more arduous path. He spent most of the next ten years pouring out a steady stream of books exploring various dimensions of what it means to be an authentic person and a true Christian. He died young—possibly of tuberculosis—totally spent by his efforts.

In Kierkegaard's philosophy most of the key existentialist themes are sounded, including freedom, individuality, authenticity, choice, commitment, dread, and despair. His central theme is that human existence is plagued by a pervasive sense of anxiety, sin, and despair, and that the only cure for this is a leap of faith and an absolute, all-in commitment to God. Making such a leap is frightening and it is not "rational," Kierkegaard believes. It requires us to stake everything on something that looks quite improbable from the standpoint of logic and common sense. This is why, in Kierkegaard's famous phrase, the life of faith is like floating on the deep over "seventy thousand fathoms" of water. For Kierkegaard, faith is not a stasis, a calm oasis in the desert. It is a constantly renewed recommitment, a leap into the dark that seems crazy by the world's standards. Thus, only in the transcendent is there true respite from anxiety and dread.

> For Kierkegaard,
> faith is not a stasis,
> a calm oasis
> in the desert.
> It is a constantly
> renewed
> recommitment,
> a leap into
> the dark.

SEE ALSO Truth Is Subjectivity (1846), Existential Defiance (1942), Atheistic Existentialism (1946)

TRUTH IS
SUBJECTIVITY

Søren Kierkegaard (1813–55)

ONE OF KIERKEGAARD'S MOST FAMOUS SAYINGS is that "truth is sub-jectivity." He did not mean that truth is just a matter of opinion or that it is okay to believe whatever you want. He meant something much deeper.

Kierkegaard's idea of truth as subjectivity is connected with his view of faith. For Kierkegaard, faith is not a matter of accepting revealed truths on the authority of the Church or the Bible. Faith is a leap, a passionate commitment of one's whole self, to something that appears absurd from the standpoint of objective reason. Jesus said "I am the truth." Thus, for a Christian existentialist like Kierkegaard, faith and truth are ultimately the same thing: "An objective uncertainty, held fast in an appropriation-process of the most passionate inwardness, is the truth, the highest truth attainable for an existing individual."

In his greatest book, *Concluding Unscientific Postscript* (1846), Kierkegaard made an important distinction between "having the truth" and "being in the truth." Someone who knows all the important truths about religion but makes no effort to live up to them "has" the truth in the sense that he can reel off correct answers on a theology test. But what is far more important is to be "in" the truth by making those religious beliefs operational in one's life. According to Kierkegaard, attempts to reach God by objective reasoning are bound to fail. And even if we could make God an object of objective knowledge, what good would it do us without the reality of a living faith? As Kierkegaard saw it, the really important thing in religion is the quality of the *relationship* one has with God. When we focus on objective knowledge, we concentrate on the object, on whether the searchlight of our minds, so to speak, has hit upon the right thing. But when it comes to God, what matters most is whether we have related ourselves to Him in the right way. Have I taken up the reality of the saving God into my life with the "passionate inwardness" true faith demands? This is the central question Kierkegaard poses for his religious readers.

OPPOSITE: Sketch of Søren Kierkegaard by his second cousin, artist Niels Christian Kierkegaard, c. 1840.

SEE ALSO Existentialism (1843), *I and Thou* (1923)

WALDEN

Henry David Thoreau (1817–62)

WAS THOREAU A PHILOSOPHER? Certainly he was a lover of wisdom, which is what the term originally meant to the ancient Greeks. Thoreau himself stated: "To be a philosopher is not merely to have subtle thoughts, nor even to found a school, but so to love wisdom as to live according to its dictates, a life of simplicity, independence, magnanimity and trust." By this definition, Thoreau was a philosopher of the first rank.

Born in Concord, Massachusetts, Thoreau spent nearly his whole life there, making ends meet by surveying, making pencils, and occasionally lecturing. His true life was lived in the fields and woods as a "self-appointed inspector of snow-storms and rain-storms." In his late twenties, he spent twenty-six months in a small cabin he built on the shore of Walden Pond. Out of that experience, he distilled one of the enduring masterpieces of American literature, *Walden* (1854). Like Ralph Waldo Emerson, Thoreau was a transcendentalist who believed that there was a divine element in every human being, that through this element we can intuit moral and spiritual truths, and that nature was a mirror and symbol of the divine. As a Romantic, Thoreau believed in people's innate goodness and agreed with William Wordsworth about the beneficent moral "impulses" emanating from smiling meadows and sun-dappled woods. As he saw it, "all good things are wild, and free."

Thoreau's essay "Civil Disobedience" (1849) was a major influence on Mahatma Gandhi's anticolonial liberation movement in India and on Martin Luther King Jr.'s campaign of nonviolent protest during the American civil-rights era. Thoreau was among the first to suggest the creation of a national park system, and his writings strongly impacted John Muir (1838–1914) and other key figures in the American environmental

A daguerreotype of Henry David Thoreau
taken by Benjamin Dexter Maxham in 1856.

movement. Today he acts as an inspiration to the contemporary voluntary simplicity movement, which is sure to grow as we confront the challenges of climate change. Though he died young, he led a life "rich in sunny hours and summer days." He will always speak to those who need "the tonic of wildness" and believe that the true cost of anything is the amount of "life which is required to be exchanged for it."

SEE ALSO Cynicism (c. 400 BCE), The Birth of Romanticism (c. 1760), American Transcendentalism (1836)

ON LIBERTY

John Stuart Mill (1806–73)

OVER THE COURSE OF HUMAN HISTORY, threats to individual liberty have come mainly from tyrants, conquerors, and oppressive elites. In *On Liberty* (1859), English philosopher and political theorist John Stuart Mill

Photograph of John Stuart Mill, c. 1870.

focuses on a relatively new threat to freedom: the "tyranny of the majority." Though widely denounced in Mill's own day, *On Liberty* is now generally recognized as one of the great classics of political philosophy.

The central thesis of *On Liberty* is that society can legitimately restrict individual liberty only in order to prevent one person from harming another. This proposed standard, now called the harm principle, has far-reaching implications. Historically, nearly all societies have had laws that banned conduct simply because it was considered to be offensive, immoral, irreligious, or harmful to oneself. The harm principle excludes all such laws. Only behavior that harms, or threatens harm to, other people can be outlawed or otherwise restricted. Mill argues for the harm principle not by appealing to individual rights or human dignity, but on utilitarian grounds. Specifically, Mill argues that respect for individual liberty is vital to social progress and the full development of one's individuality and higher capacities.

On Liberty also contains a powerful defense of freedom of thought and expression. A censored opinion, Mill notes, can be entirely true, partly true, or completely false. By censoring an opinion that is wholly or partly true, we lose the chance to replace error with truth. Even completely false opinions should not be censored, Mill argues, because truths that are protected from all critical scrutiny often fossilize into mere dogmas or meaningless formulae. Mill was a bold thinker, far ahead of his time on issues such as women's rights and participatory democracy. When *On Liberty* was first published, it was widely considered a tissue of radical nonsense that threatened the very foundations of social order. Today we live in an increasingly Millian world. Many nations have liberalized their laws on same-sex marriage, physician-assisted suicide, adultery, recreational drug use, pornography, gambling, prostitution, and other so-called "morals offenses." Mill's *On Liberty* has been a seminal text in this process.

SEE ALSO Political Libertarianism (1974)

SOCIAL DARWINISM

Herbert Spencer (1820–1903)

WHEN CHARLES DARWIN'S *ON THE ORIGIN OF SPECIES* was published in 1859, it sent shock waves through almost every field of human thought. In the natural sciences, theology, philosophy, history, and many other disciplines, there were intense efforts to explore the implications of evolution. One effort along these lines was what later came to be called social Darwinism: basically the attempt to apply the lessons of biological evolution to human societies. In nature, it was claimed, progress occurs through a ruthless process of competitive struggle and "survival of the fittest." In a similar way, human progress will occur only if government allows unrestricted business competition and makes no effort to protect the "weak" and "unfit" by means of social welfare laws.

> [Spencer] argued that there is a general law of evolutionary progress that applies . . . to human individuals and societies as well.

The most influential defender of social Darwinism was the British philosopher and social scientist Herbert Spencer. In 1862, Spencer published *First Principles*, the first volume of his massive ten-volume series titled System of Synthetic Philosophy (1862–93). In this series, he argued that there is a general law of evolutionary progress that applies not only to nature, but to human individuals and societies as well.

Though largely forgotten today, Spencer was hugely influential in the late nineteenth century, especially in the United States. Spencer's gospel of progress through struggle and competition struck a nerve in the heady "Gilded Age" of postbellum America.

By the 1890s, social Darwinism was in rapid decline. Critics pointed out that there is no scientific basis for any general law of "evolutionary progress" that reigns at every level of nature and human affairs. They also noted that moral lessons—such as how societies should treat the old or mentally handicapped—cannot be drawn by looking to nature, which is indifferent to moral values. Finally, many people began to see firsthand the toll that unrestricted competition in the industrial age took on ordinary people's lives and the environment. As the Progressive Era dawned, increasing numbers of Americans came to believe that government has a legitimate role to play in addressing social problems such as child labor, safe working conditions, old-age insurance, maximum working hours, monopolistic pricing, and environmental destruction.

SEE ALSO Political Libertarianism (1974)

REFINED UTILITARIANISM

John Stuart Mill (1806–73)

MILL'S *UTILITARIANISM*, first published in *Fraser's Magazine* in London in 1861 and then as a book in 1863, is a landmark in ethics. Although there had been defenders of utilitarianism since at least the end of the eighteenth century, it was Mill's book that made it arguably the leading ethical theory in English-speaking countries. Mill was able to accomplish this by refining utilitarianism in ways that made it less at odds with popular morality.

In his youth, Mill had been an ardent disciple of Jeremy Bentham, the most important early defender of utilitarianism. Bentham argued that pleasure is the only thing people ever desire for its own sake and that there are no higher or lower pleasures. Mill rejects both of these claims.

Like Bentham, Mill equates pleasure with happiness and claims that happiness is the only thing people ever desire as an end. But he softens what many saw as Bentham's crude psychology by maintaining that other sorts of goods, such as friendship, knowledge, and virtue, can be desired as *parts* of happiness, or as constitutive of a person's conception of happiness. He also claims that pleasures differ in quality as well as quantity. Like most Victorians, Mill believed that mental pleasures have higher value than pleasures of the body, and that anyone who had experienced both sorts of pleasures would prefer those of the mind.

Mill modifies Bentham's utilitarianism in other ways as well. One was to give a greater place to conventional moral rules. Bentham seemed to hold that rules like "don't lie" and "keep your promises" should play little or no role in moral decision making. Mill disagrees. While he concurs with Bentham that the principle of utility is the ultimate test of moral rightness, he also believes that following moral rules is usually the best strategy for maximizing long-term happiness. Only when moral rules conflict is it necessary to appeal to the principle of utility directly.

Mill succeeded in getting his contemporaries to give utilitarianism a serious hearing. After 150 years, *Utilitarianism* remains as one of the most influential and widely read books on ethics.

> Mill [maintains] that other sorts of goods, such as friendship, knowledge, and virtue, can be desired as parts of happiness.

SEE ALSO Cyrenaic Hedonism (c. 400 BCE), Epicureanism (c. 300 BCE), Utilitarianism (1789), *A Theory of Justice* (1971)

ORIGINS OF PRAGMATISM

Charles Sanders Peirce (1839–1914)

C. S. PEIRCE WAS A NEGLECTED GENIUS during his lifetime but is now widely regarded as one of America's greatest philosophers. He made important contributions to logic, science, and the philosophy of language, but he is best known as the inventor of pragmatism. He first introduced the idea of pragmatism in an 1878 paper titled "How to Make Our Ideas Clear."

Peirce believed there is a close connection between thought and action. The whole function of thought, he said, is to produce habits of actions. We find ourselves irritated by doubts, uncertain what to believe or do. The goal of thought is to remove these annoyances, to achieve rest through settled belief. Because of the close connection between thought and action, we can achieve maximum clarity in our ideas by unpacking what we take to be the practical consequences of those ideas. In fact, Peirce goes so far as to say our "idea of anything *is* our idea of its sensible effects." This provides the basis for Peirce's pragmatic theory of meaning, which holds that the meaning of an idea is the sum total of its conceived practical consequences.

Peirce's pragmatic theory of meaning has two important implications for the practice of philosophy. First, if two allegedly different ideas have exactly the same practical consequences, they are really the same idea. As an example, Peirce cites the alleged difference between Catholic and Protestant views of the Eucharist. Catholics say that the consecrated bread and wine are no longer bread and wine but have been miraculously transformed into the body and blood of Christ. Protestants reject this doctrine of literal transubstantiation. But do Catholics and Protestants disagree about any of the practical effects of their respective views of the Eucharist? If not, then their disagreement is merely verbal, not real.

The second important implication of Peirce's pragmatic theory of meaning is that ideas and theories that have *no* conceivable practical implications are meaningless. As a hardheaded working scientist, Peirce was not impressed by airy theorizing. In proposing a pragmatic theory of meaning, Peirce hoped to make philosophy more practical and more like science.

Steel engraving of Christ with bread and wine at the Last Supper, 1836, after *The Redeemer* by Italian painter Carlo Dolci (1616–86). Peirce cites the Catholic and Protestant views of the Eucharist as exemplifying his pragmatic theory that two allegedly different ideas with the same practical consequences are really the same idea.

SEE ALSO *Pragmatism* (1907), Instrumentalism (1925)

"GOD IS DEAD"

Friedrich Nietzsche (1844–1900)

IN TWO OF HIS BOOKS, *The Gay Science* (or *Joyful Wisdom*) (1882) and *Thus Spake Zarathustra* (1883–85), the important nineteenth-century German philosopher Friedrich Nietzsche dramatically declares that "God is dead." This is one of the most famous sayings in philosophy, but what does it mean?

A c. 1910 drawing created from an iconic photograph of Friedrich Nietzsche.

Nietzsche does not, of course, mean that God has literally died—that once God existed, but he has since expired. Nor does he mean, as some have suggested, that authentic belief in God is no longer possible. As he explains in *The Gay Science,* what he means is that God is now "unworthy of belief" in the sense that belief in God has been discredited. There are no longer any rational grounds for affirming that God exists. How did this occur? "We have killed him," Nietzsche says. In his view, all the traditional arguments for God's existence have been thoroughly undermined by science, philosophy, modern biblical criticism, and other corrosive developments in the modern world. Yet Nietzsche notes that "this tremendous event . . . has not yet reached the ears of man." It has not yet truly sunk in, either to the masses or even to most intellectuals. When it does, Nietzsche predicts, the effects will be both calamitous and (for "free spirits") a cause for joy.

Nietzsche does not believe we can give up belief in God and just continue on our merry way; we must also give up all belief in objective moral values, objective meanings, and even objective truth. When the full ramifications of God's death sink in, all traditional moorings will be lost. It will be as though a sponge has "wipe[d] away the entire horizon," the Earth has been "unchained" from the sun, and there is no longer "any up or down." Unprecedented wars and violence will break out, and the whole structure of Christian civilization will be destroyed.

Despite this sense of apocalyptic foreboding, Nietzsche saw a bright side to the death of God. With no "anti-life," sin-obsessed God to impose values and meanings, strong, clear-eyed "free spirits" will at last be free to create their life-affirming values and meanings, and an exciting new world will open up.

SEE ALSO Perspectivism (1882), The Revaluation of Values (1887), Atheistic Existentialism (1946)

PERSPECTIVISM

Friedrich Nietzsche (1844–1900)

NIETZSCHE USES THE TERM *PERSPECTIVISM* to describe his general view of truth and knowledge. Exactly what Nietzsche's perspectivism amounts to is one of the most vexing questions in Nietzsche scholarship, but certain features of his view are clear.

First, Nietzsche views reality as a chaotic flux of "becoming" that we turn into something intelligible by imposing categories such as thing, substance, permanence, object, cause, and attribute. The world, he tells us, "is a mere fiction, constructed of fictitious entities." It follows that there is no perspective-independent "real world" and that there cannot be any objective or absolute truths in the sense of beliefs or statements that correspond to "the way things really are," independent of human perceptions and categorizations. "There are no facts," as he famously puts it, "only interpretations."

> Nietzsche believed that . . . as individuals, we adopt various interpretations of reality as "a means of becoming master over something."

Second, Nietzsche supports his perspectivist view by connecting it to his idea of "the will to power." Nietzsche believed that human beings, and indeed all forms of life, are driven by a restless desire to survive, to grow, to enlarge and discharge their powers, and to dominate others. Inevitably, Nietzsche argues, the will to power shapes the way we perceive reality. As a species, we have adopted a commonsense worldview as divided into more or less enduring "things" because we have found this useful in the struggle for survival. As individuals, we adopt various interpretations of reality as "a means of becoming master over something." All seeing and knowing is thus seeing and knowing from a certain vantage point that is significantly shaped by the will to power. Therefore, even if there were a "real world," there could be no objective or perspective-free knowledge of it, because all human attempts to make sense of the world must operate through "lenses" that are fashioned by our will-to-power-driven interests, needs, values, and so forth. These, of course, vary from person to person and culture to culture.

Nietzsche never worked out his perspectivism into a clear and systematic theory. What he does say raises lots of fascinating questions. Many twentieth-century postmodernists, pragmatists, and feminists were influenced by Nietzsche's perspectivism and developed his ideas in various directions.

SEE ALSO "God Is Dead" (1882), The Revaluation of Values (1887), Power/Knowledge (1975), Postmodernism (1979)

THE REVALUATION OF VALUES

Friedrich Nietzsche (1844–1900)

NIETZSCHE WAS AN ICONOCLAST about ethics. He denied that there are any moral facts, rejected the idea of any objective or universal moral standards, and argued for a "revaluation of all values" in light of the "death of God." He often described himself as an "immoralist" for his radically unconventional views. Just what did Nietzsche's immoralism amount to?

In his sketchy but fascinating 1887 "history" of morals, *On the Genealogy of Morality*, Nietzsche identifies two types of morality: master morality and slave morality. In ancient times, particularly in Homeric Greece and during periods of Roman history, the dominant morality was master morality. This was a noble, aristocratic ethical code that prized virtues like courage, strength, cunning, pride, self-confidence, love of life, love of beauty, self-overcoming, and contempt for the inferior herd.

As Nietzsche tells it, this master morality was attacked and largely replaced by a greatly inferior approach to ethics that he calls slave morality or herd morality. Examples of slave morality include Judeo-Christian ethics and utilitarianism. Slave morality is designed to protect "the herd," that is, the weak and powerless, from exploitation by the strong. For this reason, it prizes virtues that smooth social life and promote collective happiness like kindness, humility, pity, benevolence, meekness, hard work, law-abidingness, justice, and equality. Because of the long dominance of Christianity, slave morality in the West also has long-valued religious virtues such as chastity, self-denial, anxious concern for the purity of one's thoughts, contrition, hostility to pleasure and to the senses, and generally a preoccupation with the next life and a contempt for this one.

When Nietzsche says that we should "revaluate all values," what he mainly means is that we should thoroughly reexamine prevailing slave-morality ethical standards. Many of those standards, he believed, make no sense once we recognize that there is no God and no afterlife. For the strong, what Nietzsche calls "us free spirits," maybe some of the old master morality values would be more life-affirming and lead to greater forms of excellence. With God out of the picture, he says in *The Gay Science* (1882), the horizon at long last "appears free to us again." "The sea, our sea, lies open again; perhaps there has never been such an 'open sea.'"

> Many [slave-morality ethical] standards, he believed, make no sense once we recognize that there is no God and no afterlife.

SEE ALSO "God Is Dead" (1882), Perspectivism (1882)

"THE WILL TO BELIEVE"

William James (1842–1910)

WILLIAM JAMES'S "THE WILL TO BELIEVE" is probably the most widely read essay on the ethics of belief ever written. It has been both widely praised and widely criticized, and it has been interpreted in sharply conflicting ways.

In some ways, James's argument can be seen as a new and improved version of Pascal's famous wager argument for belief in God. Pascal argued that we should "bet" that God exists, even if it seems highly unlikely that he does, because we have everything to gain if we bet right and little or nothing to lose if we bet wrong. James rejects Pascal's argument, mainly because it licenses a kind of wishful thinking that James believes is both morally and intellectually indefensible. According to James, however, something close to Pascal's Wager, suitably modified, can be defended.

> In some ways, James's argument can be seen as a new and improved version of Pascal's famous wager argument for belief in God.

James's basic strategy is to drastically limit the kinds of cases in which Pascal-like appeals to self-interest are legitimate. James imposes two kinds of restrictions: First, the choice between the relevant betting options must be intellectually undecidable. That is, there cannot be compelling evidence in favor of either option. Second, the choice must be what James calls a "genuine option." A genuine option, as James defines it, is one that is "momentous" (has great personal significance), "living" (you could sincerely believe or disbelieve it), and "forced" (you have to "bet," whether you wish to or not). James argues that, for many people, belief in God (or what he somewhat nebulously calls "the religious hypothesis") meets all these conditions. Such people, James argues, have an intellectual and moral right to believe in God even though they have no compelling evidence that he exists.

James's argument was directed in part against certain militant agnostics of his day, including the English mathematician William Kingdon Clifford (1845–79), who boldly pronounced that "it is wrong always, everywhere, and for anyone to believe anything on insufficient evidence." Whether James succeeds or not in showing that there is a right to believe in God in the face of inconclusive evidence, his essay raises fascinating questions about intellectual standards and the role that evidence should play in forming our beliefs and our ultimate commitments.

SEE ALSO Pascal's Wager (1670)

PHENOMENOLOGY

Edmund Husserl (1859–1938)

PROBABLY THE TWO MOST IMPORTANT developments in twentieth-century philosophy were the emergence of analytic philosophy and phenomenology. Edmund Husserl was the father of phenomenology, and for this reason he is one of the most important philosophers of the last century.

Husserl was born in Prossnitz (Prostejeov), in what is now the Czech Republic; his family was Jewish, though Husserl later became a Protestant. Trained as a mathematician, Husserl switched to philosophy after studying with Franz Brentano (1838–1917) in the mid-1880s at the University of Vienna. Husserl went on to teach philosophy at various German universities, including Göttingen and Freiburg. His most important work, *Logical Investigations*, was published in two volumes in 1900–1901. Later books, such as *Ideas* (1913), *Formal and Transcendental Logic* (1929), and *The Crisis of European Sciences and Transcendental Phenomenology* (1936), refined his phenomenological method, sometimes in ways that branched off in quite new directions from his earlier thought.

Husserl believed that philosophy should be a strict science and based on ideas that are absolutely certain. Like Descartes, Husserl found his crucial starting point in our own conscious awareness. Philosophy, he argued, should employ the method of phenomenology. Essentially, this means a careful and precise introspective study of mental phenomena (sensations, concepts, feelings, imagined objects, etc.), without presupposing that any objects of awareness actually exist outside the mind. As Husserl famously put it, for philosophical purposes we should "bracket" the whole issue of whether our minds grasp true reality and focus instead on how reality *appears* to us. This allows philosophy to draw conclusions that are 100 percent certain, even if

A photograph of Edmund Husserl, c. 1910s.

skeptics are right that what we call reality might be some kind of illusion. Like Brentano, Husserl believed that all thought is "intentional," that is, directed toward some object. We can thus distinguish the object of thought (what Husserl called the *noema*) from the act of consciousness itself (the *noesis*). Both aspects of consciousness can be studied phenomenologically. When we do so, we discover "essences" that express necessary features of acts and objects of consciousness. For Husserl, phenomenology is primarily concerned with the study of essences and of the most general features of human thought.

SEE ALSO *Meditations on First Philosophy* (1641), *Being and Time* (1927), *Nausea* (1938)

ETHICAL INTUITIONISM

George Edward Moore (1873–1958)

ENGLISH PHILOSOPHER G. E. MOORE is one of the giants of twentieth-century philosophy. Together with Bertrand Russell, he launched a powerful campaign against idealism and in favor of realism. In epistemology, Moore argued vigorously for a "commonsense" approach to questions of knowledge. His method of doing philosophy by means of clear and painstaking conceptual analysis did much to inspire modern analytic philosophy. And in moral philosophy, his 1903 book *Principia Ethica* served as a foundational text for twentieth-century ethics.

Born in Upper Norwood, London, Moore studied classics and philosophy at Trinity College, Cambridge, where he later taught for most of his career. Among his distinguished colleagues at Trinity were Russell and Ludwig Wittgenstein (1889–1951). For over a quarter of a century, Moore edited the prestigious philosophy journal *Mind*.

In *Principia Ethica*, Moore claims that the key question of ethics is: What is good? One common answer is to identify goodness with some natural property, such as pleasure or happiness. Moore argues that all naturalistic theories of this sort are false. Any attempt to equate goodness with some natural property is a mistake that Moore famously dubs the "naturalistic fallacy." (Exactly what the mistake is, or even whether it is a mistake, is disputed.) If "good" just means "pleasure," for example, then it would be true by definition to say "What is pleasurable is good," which it clearly is not. All attempts to define goodness in naturalistic terms succumb to "open question argument." No matter what definition is proposed, it will be an open question whether the definition is correct. This shows that the claimed equivalence doesn't hold.

Generalizing these arguments, Moore claims that goodness can't be defined. "Good" denotes a simple, unanalyzable, nonnatural property. So how can we determine what things are intrinsically good? By intuition: we employ a "test of isolation." Imagine if that thing were the sole reality, existing in complete isolation from anything else. Would it still be good? If so, it is intrinsically good. When we employ the test of isolation, Moore argues, we can intuit that the greatest intrinsic goods are those of personal affection and aesthetic experience. This made Moore very popular with the Bloomsbury Group of artists and writers, many of whom were Moore's friends.

> Moore claims that goodness can't be defined. "Good" denotes a simple, unanalyzable, nonnatural property.

SEE ALSO The Moral Sense (1725), Deontological Intuitionism (1930)

PRAGMATISM

William James (1842–1910)

Though pragmatism was the brainchild of C. S. Peirce, it was first popularized by William James in his 1907 book *Pragmatism: A New Name for Some Old Ways of Thinking*. Like Peirce, James embraced a pragmatic theory of meaning. Expanding on an article by Peirce published in *Popular Science Monthly* in January 1878, James writes:

> To attain perfect clearness in our thoughts of an object . . . we need only consider what conceivable effects of a practical kind the object may involve—what sensations we are to expect from it, and what reactions we must prepare. Our conception of these effects, whether immediate or remote, is then for us the whole of our conception of the object, so far as that conception has positive significance at all.

In this sense, pragmatism is a method of clarifying our ideas and also a method of settling philosophical disputes that might otherwise be interminable. Some philosophical disputes can be dismissed as pointless, because nothing of practical significance rides on the outcome, or because on inspection they can be seen to have no practical consequences at all. So far, Peirce would agree, though with one major difference: when James talks about "practical effects," he includes personal reactions and emotional responses, whereas Peirce focuses on general ways that ideas could conceivably influence behavior.

There is another important difference between Peirce and James. For James, pragmatism is more than a theory of meaning; it is also a theory of truth. He rejects the idea of objective truth. In James's folksy metaphors, an idea is true if it "works," if it has significant "cash-value" in experiential terms. James never succeeded in making altogether clear what he means by such expressions. But it is evident that he is thinking primarily of the way certain parts of our experience can validate others. "True ideas," he writes, "are those that we can assimilate, validate, corroborate and verify." He adds: "Any idea upon which we can ride, so to speak; any idea that will carry us prosperously from any one part of our experience to any other part, linking things satisfactorily . . . is true for just so much, true in so far forth, true instrumentally."

> For James, pragmatism is more than a theory of meaning; it is also a theory of truth. He rejects the idea of objective truth.

Peirce rejected James's pragmatic theory of truth and suggested that his own version of pragmatism be renamed "pragmaticism." Such an ungainly term, he said, "is ugly enough to be safe from kidnappers."

SEE ALSO Origins of Pragmatism (1878), Instrumentalism (1925)

PROGRESSIVE EDUCATION

John Dewey (1859–1952)

SCHOOLS IN NINETEENTH-CENTURY AMERICA tended to emphasize rote learning and singsong drill. Children were treated as miniature adults by authoritarian teachers who taught them subjects that often had little connection with their home life, their community, or anything they were interested in outside of school. This began to change during the era of progressive education, which began in the late nineteenth century and reached its heyday in the 1930s and 1940s. The most important exponent of progressive education was John Dewey.

Dewey was born in Burlington, Vermont, in 1859. After receiving his PhD in philosophy from Johns Hopkins in 1884, Dewey taught philosophy and psychology at the University of Michigan, the University of Chicago, and Columbia University. A prolific but often woolly writer, Dewey published more than one thousand books and articles over his sixty-five-year career. Currently, there is a notable revival of interest in his work as a pragmatist. But Dewey's greatest influence was in the field of education.

> Dewey criticized traditional methods of education and argued for the creation of schools that were more child-centered and democratic.

Dewey wrote several books on educational theory, but his magnum opus is *Democracy and Education*, published in 1916. There, Dewey criticized traditional methods of education and argued for the creation of schools that were more child-centered and democratic; that stressed critical thinking, problem solving, and active learning by doing rather than rote memorization; that bridged the gap between school and real life; and that recognized the fundamental role education plays in social progress and democratic self-governance. The ultimate aim of education, Dewey argues, is growth. A good education is one that inspires a passion for continued learning and growth, and that equips students with the tools they need to achieve it.

Much of this is now part of the educational mainstream, incorporated into the lore of the pedagogical tribe. Critics, such as the "core knowledge" advocate E. D. Hirsch (b. 1928), charge that Dewey went too far. Hirsch argues that the main reason too many American students cannot read, write, or do basic math is that teachers have bought into a Dewey-inspired "thoughtworld" that emphasizes "critical thinking" and "learning to learn" over facts and essential knowledge. That such debates continue to be central to educational reform is a testament to the enduring influence of John Dewey.

SEE ALSO *Emile* and Natural Education (1762), Instrumentalism (1925)

I AND THOU

Martin Buber (1878–1965)

MARTIN BUBER IS ONE OF THE MOST IMPORTANT Jewish philosophers and religious thinkers of the twentieth century. Born in Vienna into an Orthodox Jewish family, Buber was strongly influenced as a youth by Kant and Nietzsche, as well as by Hasidic Judaism, a branch of Jewish mysticism

Martin Buber photographed in 1963 arriving at Amsterdam Airport; he was in the city to receive the Erasmus Prize, a prestigious Dutch award, for his work.

that arose in Eastern Europe in the eighteenth century. After teaching for many years at Frankfurt am Main, Buber moved to Israel, where he taught at Hebrew University from 1938 to 1951. In 1923, he published his most important book, *I and Thou (Ich und Du)*, which has become a modern religious classic.

According to Buber, human personhood arises from relation. There are two primary relations: the I-It and the I-Thou. The "self," or the "I," comes into existence and determines itself by the way it engages in these two primary relations. The usual way of relating to things is in the I-It mode. This is the way of using, experiencing, and observing persons and things; it is marked by a subject-object split and is instrumentalist, objectivizing, and lacking in true mutuality. While indispensable, the I-It mode of relationship is not the primary human or spiritual relationship. Real knowledge of another person must be dialogical; it requires openness, participation, empathy, and genuine encounter. This is a unique kind of personal knowledge that can never be adequately expressed by words. It is ineffable, for all speech presupposes a subject-object split, which is transcended in the holistic mutuality of the I-Thou relationship.

According to Buber, we face an existentialist and spiritual crisis today because of the increasing dominance of I-It relations. This makes impossible not only any genuine human community but also any true spiritual life. As a person, the Eternal Thou, God, cannot be known through objectifying I-It modes of relatedness. In fact, God is the one Reality that can never become an It. True openness and mutuality can never be forced. Only when we open ourselves to God and risk commitment can we encounter the Eternal Thou. Such encounters don't require any sacred places or mediating institutions, but occur whenever we embrace the sacredness of the ordinary and everyday; "if you hallow this life you meet the living God."

SEE ALSO Existentialism (1843), Existential Defiance (1942), Atheistic Existentialism (1946)

INSTRUMENTALISM

John Dewey (1859–1952)

DEWEY WAS A PRAGMATIST in the tradition of Charles Sanders Peirce and William James, but his version of pragmatism included a few new twists. Dewey called his form of pragmatism "instrumentalism" to highlight his view that ideas and theories are tools to help us make sense of reality and to cope successfully with life's challenges. The practical, instrumental function of thought is a prominent theme in Dewey's most important work, *Experience and Nature* (1925).

Unlike Peirce and James, Dewey was a naturalist who believed that nothing supernatural exists and that every aspect of human existence must be explained in naturalistic (especially biological and evolutionary) terms. Dewey was also an empiricist who refused to recognize the existence of things like objective moral values or Kantian things-in-themselves that lack a clear warrant in experience. For this reason, Dewey rejected the traditional correspondence of truth, the view that a statement or belief is true just in case it "fits the facts" or "matches up with the way reality really is." Dewey agreed with James that the idea of "the way reality really is" is an empty placeholder, because we have no way to compare our beliefs about reality with mind-independent reality itself. Like James, Dewey claimed that the only empirically warranted concept of truth is of that which "works" in human experience. True ideas are those that help us solve problems effectively, lead to higher values and meanings, and have been verified by experience. Late in life, Dewey scrapped talk of "truth" altogether and spoke instead of "warranted assertions." The term "truth," he believed, was too bound up with false metaphysical assumptions to be useful.

If truth, or "warranted assertibility," is what works, then thought has a practical function. Ideas, theories, and methods of inquiry should be seen

A painting of John Dewey, c. 1920.

as tools that may be more or less effective in helping us cope with problems and render our experience of the world richer and more coherent. In this vein, philosophy too should be regarded as a tool. Its main purpose, Dewey contended, was to contribute to the solution of practical problems and to improve the human condition.

SEE ALSO Origins of Pragmatism (1878), *Pragmatism* (1907), Progressive Education (1916)

1927

BEING AND TIME

Martin Heidegger (1889–1976)

IN 1927, MARTIN HEIDEGGER published *Being and Time*, widely recognized as one of the most important philosophical works of the twentieth century. Heidegger's penetrating analyses of such concepts as authenticity, finitude, temporality, guilt, anxiety, and care have become deeply embedded in contemporary philosophy.

For many readers, one of the most thought-provoking parts of Heidegger's philosophy is his discussion of death. Heidegger was born of peasant stock in the town of Messkirch in southwestern Germany. Educated in Jesuit schools, he trained to become a priest before deciding to leave the Church shortly after the end of World War I. From 1918 to 1923, Heidegger taught at the University of Freiburg, where he was strongly influenced by the phenomenological approach of his senior colleague Edmund Husserl. After publishing *Being and Time*, Heidegger was appointed to succeed Husserl in the chair of philosophy at Freiburg.

Following the rise of Hitler, Heidegger joined the Nazi Party; as rector of Freiburg (1933–34) he gave pro-Nazi speeches and reportedly fired Jewish professors. (The facts are disputed.) Following Germany's defeat in World War II, Heidegger was banned from teaching for several years because of his Nazi sympathies. Much of his later writing is concerned with the thought of earlier thinkers, such as Kant, Nietzsche, and the pre-Socratics. He is buried in the town cemetery of his native Messkirch.

Heidegger notes that humans relate to death differently than do other animals. We know that we will die, and in fact know that we can die at any moment. Finitude, negation, and precariousness are thus built into human existence, and our path through life is inherently a kind of "being-towards-death." For many people, death is a deeply uncomfortable and even taboo subject; our typical response is one of denial, avoidance, and an averted gaze. Moreover, it is easy to objectivize death and regard it as a fact outside ourselves; death is something that happens to "other people." Yet Heidegger argues that accepting death can enhance the human quest for meaning and authenticity. Knowing that our time on earth is limited and that each breath might be our last makes every moment precious and lends depth and "resoluteness" to our lives.

> *Being and Time* [is] widely recognized as one of the most important philosophical works of the twentieth century.

SEE ALSO Phenomenology (1900)

RELIGION
AS WISH FULFILLMENT

Sigmund Freud (1856–1939)

EVEN THOUGH SIGMUND FREUD was a psychiatrist rather than a philosopher, his influence on philosophy has been enormous. His views on the unconscious, psychoanalysis, dream interpretation, the Oedipus complex, repression, sublimation, and the constraints of civilization on humankind's unruly primitive instincts have been extensively discussed by philosophers. Though Freud's reputation has declined dramatically over the past few decades, many of his ideas have more than simply historical interest. One is his claim that religion is an illusion rooted in wishful thinking.

> Freud writes, "religiousness is to be traced to the small human child's long-drawn-out helplessness and need of help."

Freud defends this view of religion most fully in his short, hard-hitting book *The Future of an Illusion* (1927). Earlier thinkers, most notably German philosopher and anthropologist Ludwig Feuerbach (1804–72), had argued that God is a projection of idealized human traits and that religious belief results from human fears and wishes. Freud supplements Feuerbach's critique with a psychological explanation drawn from his own theory of childhood development.

Freud was an atheist who thought that belief in God rested on "feeble grounds" and was "patently infantile." Why is it then that so many intelligent people continue to hold religious beliefs? Freud's answer is that religion survives because it is rooted in something deeper and more primal than reason: human wishes and fears. As Freud sees it, religion gets much of its psychological grip from events in our childhood. "Biologically speaking," Freud writes, "religiousness is to be traced to the small human child's long-drawn-out helplessness and need of help." As children, we're grateful for the protection of our parents, particularly our strong, loving fathers, who can somehow make everything come out all right. As adults, we also confront fears and insecurities. We find ourselves in a cold, implacable world; we hunger for meaning, security, consolation, justice, life beyond the grave. These deep-seated wishes and fears, Freud suggests, explain why so many cling to religion, despite its lack of rational support.

Freud's psychological explanation of religion has drawn many responses. One of the most interesting was offered by C. S. Lewis (1898–1963), the noted Christian apologist and author. Lewis suggested that even if religion is rooted in wishful thinking (which he denied), God might have implanted in us a deep desire for Himself. In that case, wishful thinking might be one of God's ways of leading us home.

SEE ALSO "God Is Dead" (1882), The New Atheists (2004)

DEONTOLOGICAL INTUITIONISM

William David Ross (1877–1971)

IN THE EARLY DECADES of the twentieth century, utilitarianism was the dominant ethical theory in Anglo-American philosophy. However, there were powerful critics of utilitarianism. One of the most important was the Oxford classical scholar W. D. Ross. He was the leading Aristotle scholar of his day, but he also made significant contributions to ethics. In his two major works on ethics, *The Right and the Good* (1930) and *Foundations of Ethics* (1939), Ross lays out an attractive form of deontological, or duty-centered, ethics. Unlike Kant's deontological ethics, which claims that there is only one basic moral principle, Ross argues that there are a cluster of fundamental ethical principles. These basic moral principles are "immediately apprehended," or intuited, by all persons of developed moral consciousness. For this reason, Ross's theory is a form of deontological intuitionism.

Ross claims that reflection on moral experience reveals that there are seven basic moral duties: fidelity (telling the truth, keeping promises, etc.); reparation (making up for a harm one has done); gratitude (repaying a kindness); justice (distributing goods fairly and treating people as they deserve); beneficence (doing good); self-improvement (striving to be a better person); and nonmaleficence (not injuring others). Sometimes these duties conflict. For example, by keeping a promise, I might wrongly harm someone. No duty is absolute; all have exceptions. All basic moral principles, therefore, state only what Ross calls "prima facie duties." They specify actual moral obligations only if they are not overridden by more weighty duties.

Like Aristotle, Ross denies that there is any simple recipe for making good moral decisions. Ethics is too complicated to be reduced to an algorithm or a catchphrase. Still, many critics have complained that Ross's ethical theory is not terribly helpful. How do we know that there are seven, and only seven, basic moral duties? By intuition. How do we decide which of two conflicting prima facie moral duties is more important? By intuition. This prompted British ethicist G. J. Warnock (1923–95) to complain that Ross's theory "seems deliberately, almost perversely, to answer no questions, to throw no light on any problem." This may be excessively harsh, but does point to a real weakness in Ross's ethics.

Ross claims that reflection on moral experience reveals that there are seven basic moral duties. . . . Sometimes these duties conflict.

SEE ALSO The Categorical Imperative (1785), Ethical Intuitionism (1903)

1936

LOGICAL POSITIVISM

Alfred Jules Ayer (1910–89)

MANY PHILOSOPHICAL MOVEMENTS in the twentieth century shared a modest, deflationary view of the proper role of philosophy. One such movement was logical positivism. In Anglo-American philosophy, the chief representative of logical positivism was the English philosopher A. J. Ayer.

Ayer was born in London and educated at Eton and Christ Church, Oxford. From 1932 to 1933, he lived in Vienna, where he studied with

A photochrom of the University of Vienna, from c. 1900, the stomping ground of the Vienna Circle, whom Ayer studied with from 1932 to 1933.

members of the Vienna Circle, a group of like-minded philosophers, scientists, and mathematicians who rejected metaphysics and embraced a militant form of empiricism much influenced by David Hume. Members of the Vienna Circle described themselves as logical positivists. The core doctrine of logical positivism was a revolutionary principle known as the "verifiability criterion of meaning." According to this principle, all meaningful statements about reality must in some way be verifiable through observation or experience. The logical positivists wielded the verification principle like a double-sided battle-ax to hew down whole forests of what they saw as metaphysical, theological, and ethical nonsense.

When Ayer returned to London in 1933, he began work on a book that would introduce logical positivism to English-speaking philosophers. The book, titled *Language, Truth and Logic*, was published in January 1936. Brash, hard-hitting, and beautifully written, it remains the classic manifesto of logical positivism. The book made a splash not only for its complete rejection of metaphysics and theology, but also for its uncompromising defense of an "emotivist" view of ethics. According to Ayer, ethical statements such as "Stealing money is wrong" cannot be literally true or false and in fact are "cognitively meaningless." Their purpose is not to state facts but to express and arouse feelings.

Later in his distinguished career, Ayer conceded that there were serious problems with some aspects of logical positivism. Critics noted, for example, that the verification principle cannot be verified according to its own lights. However, in the heady days following publication of *Language, Truth and Logic*, Ayer was brimming with self-confidence. When asked what he would do next, Ayer mischievously replied "There's no next. Philosophy has come to an end. Finished."

SEE ALSO *A Treatise of Human Nature* (1739), The Problem of Induction (1739)

1938

NAUSEA

Jean-Paul Sartre (1905–80)

JEAN-PAUL SARTRE is one of the few philosophers who produced both first-rate work aimed at professional philosophers and literary works such as novels, plays, and essays that enjoy wide popular acclaim. Sartre was the leading representative of existentialism following World War II. One of his most powerful literary presentations of existentialist themes is in his 1938 novel, *Nausea*.

Sartre was born in Paris, where he experienced a lonely and unhappy childhood. After training at the École normale supériere to be a teacher, Sartre taught philosophy at various schools in Le Havre, Laon, and Paris. In 1929, Sartre met Simone de Beauvoir (1908–86), who became his lifelong partner despite many "contingent loves." Bored with his work as a teacher, Sartre began writing in the mid-1930s and within a decade had become one of the best-known authors in France. His masterwork, *Being and Nothingness* (1943), offers an analysis of consciousness and "Being" (reality, existence) utilizing the phenomenological method of Edmund Husserl. After the war, Sartre became increasingly active in Marxism and radical French politics.

The main character in *Nausea* is Antoine Roquentin, a thirty-year-old writer and intellectual. Friendless and out of touch with his family, Roquentin is living in Bouville (Mud Town) writing a biography of an obscure eighteenth-century nobleman. One day while walking at the waterfront, Roquentin picks up a pebble to throw in the sea. He looks closely at it and feels a wave of disgust at its bare existence. As time passes, he finds himself increasingly overwhelmed by feelings of nausea, vertigo, anxiety, and depression. One day, when staring at the gnarled, slug-like roots of a chestnut tree, he realizes that what is causing these feelings is existence itself. As an atheistic existentialist, Roquentin sees reality as absurd, meaningless,

Jean-Paul Sartre speaking at the Faculdade Nacional de Filosofia (National College of Philosophy) at the Universidade do Brasil, 1967.

irrational, *de trop* (unwelcome), and radically contingent. As the book closes, Roquentin sits in a café listening to a favorite song. He feels a stab of joy and realizes that in art there is a productive freedom that transcends the contingency of existence and allows one to partially wash away "the sin of existing." He abandons the biography he has been working on and thinks about writing a novel.

SEE ALSO Phenomenology (1900), Existential Defiance (1942), Atheistic Existentialism (1946)

EXISTENTIAL DEFIANCE

Albert Camus (1913–60)

ALBERT CAMUS WAS A NOVELIST, playwright, essayist, and journalist. Was he also a philosopher? He denied it, saying his work was in some ways an attack on philosophy. Yet he published two nonfiction books—*The Myth of Sisyphus* (1942) and *The Rebel* (1951)—that engage closely with the works of Kierkegaard, Nietzsche, Sartre, and other philosophers, and he expounds at length what Sartre called an "absurdist philosophy" of life. Whatever label one attaches to him, Camus's ideas are worth discussing both for their intrinsic interest and for the impact they had on philosophical discussions in the aftermath of World War II.

Camus was born in Algiers, North Africa, and grew up in poverty after his father was killed in World War I. In 1942, he published a novel, *The Stranger*, which became a classic of existentialist literature. Two other major novels followed: *The Plague* (1947) and *The Fall* (1956). In 1957, he won the Nobel Prize in Literature. He died in a traffic accident in 1960 at age forty-six.

> Camus believed that human existence is absurd because the universe is indifferent and fails to satisfy unquenchable human desires.

As a philosopher, Camus is best remembered for his passionate and insightful discussions of the meaning of life and "the absurd." As an atheist, Camus believed that human existence is absurd because the universe is indifferent and fails to satisfy unquenchable human desires for hope, justice, meaning, and escape from death. This does not mean, however, that we must yield to despair. Camus referred to the Greek legend of Sisyphus, who was condemned by the gods to spend all eternity rolling a rock up a hill, only to have it roll back to the bottom over and over again. Like Sisyphus, our lives are full of labor and futile strivings that ultimately come to nothing. But we need not accept our fate; we can revolt. In Camus's retelling of the myth, Sisyphus triumphs over the gods by finding joy and meaning in the hopeless labor to which he has been condemned. He scorns the gods, says yes to life, and lives passionately in full consciousness of the futility of all things. In this way, Sisyphus becomes the "absurd hero" and a model of how brave men and women should live and die in a godless universe.

SEE ALSO "God Is Dead" (1882), Perspectivism (1882), Existentialism (1843), *Nausea* (1938), Atheistic Existentialism (1946)

ATHEISTIC EXISTENTIALISM

Jean-Paul Sartre (1905–80)

ON OCTOBER 29, 1945, the French philosopher Jean-Paul Sartre gave a lecture titled "Existentialism Is a Humanism" before a jam-packed audience at Club Maintenant in postwar Paris. Public interest in the talk was so intense that chairs were broken and some people fainted in the overcrowded club. Published as a book in 1946 and in English translation in 1947, the lecture became a foundational text in existentialist literature.

Sartre begins by noting that there are two main camps of existentialists, Christian (e.g., Kierkegaard and French philosopher Gabriel Marcel [1889–1973]) and atheistic (e.g., Heidegger). Sartre announces that he is firmly in the atheistic camp and fleshes out what his brand of atheistic existentialism entails. First, if God doesn't exist, then humans are "condemned to be free" and can't escape responsibility for their choices by making excuses. If there is no God, then there is no preordained essence to which we must conform; for humans, "existence precedes essence." We create our own essence by choosing how to live. Moreover, if God doesn't exist, there can't be any objective values in a heaven of ideas; we must choose our own values to live by. Recognizing these facts makes us "forlorn." We feel abandoned in a world without religious consolations or rules.

We also feel "anguished" because even though we are free and choose our own values, no rational agent can make a purely individual value choice. As Kant noted, moral judgments are universal in the sense that what is right for person A must also be right for any person who is in person A's exact situation. This creates an anguished sense of deep responsibility when we realize that in choosing to be a certain sort of person we are also, in effect, creating an image of how others ought to be.

Finally, Sartre's brand of atheistic existentialism leads to "despair." By this, Sartre means a kind of Stoic refusal to depend on anything that one cannot fully control. If people are totally free, then they can change overnight. This negates the possibility of deep human solidarity and trust. "I've got to limit myself to what I see" and (as Descartes said) seek to "conquer myself" rather than the world.

> If God doesn't exist, there can't be any objective values in a heaven of ideas; we must choose our own values to live by.

SEE ALSO *Meditations on First Philosophy* (1641), The Categorical Imperative (1785), "God Is Dead" (1882), Existentialism (1843), *Being and Time* (1927), Existential Defiance (1942)

THE SECOND SEX

Simone de Beauvoir (1908–86)

ONCE WIDELY SEEN AS A MERE SATELLITE of her longtime companion, Jean-Paul Sartre, Simone de Beauvoir is now considered a major thinker
and a significant philosopher in her own right. Her two-volume 1949 book,
The Second Sex, has been described by academic feminist Camille Paglia (b.
1947) as "the supreme work of modern feminism."

Beauvoir was born in Paris, the eldest child of middle-class parents, and
raised as a devout Catholic. She was an avid reader as a child and became
an atheist at age fourteen. For many years, she taught philosophy at French
secondary schools before becoming a full-time writer during World War
II. In 1929, she became romantically involved with Sartre, a close but non-
exclusive relationship that continued until Sartre's death. She never married or had children, vowing as a young woman that "whatever happened,
I would have to try to preserve what was best in me: my love of personal
freedom, my passion for life, my curiosity, my determination to be a writer."

Over a long career, Beauvoir published dozens of books, including a
highly regarded autobiography, a major work on existentialist ethics, and
the novel *The Mandarins*, which won the prestigious Prix Goncourt prize
in 1954. Her most influential work, however, is *The Second Sex*, a sprawling
eight-hundred-page analysis and deconstruction of the history of women's
oppression. In exploring "the pervasiveness and intensity and mysterious-
ness" of women's subordination, Beauvoir draws upon an amazing variety
of insights from biology, sociology, psychoanalysis, history, literature, economics, existentialism, phenomenology, and Marxism. Throughout the
work, she argues that gender is a social construction ("one is not born, but
rather becomes, woman"). Her defense of abortion, frank discussions of
women's sexuality, and uncompromising critique of marriage ("marriage

kills love") scandalized conventional readers in her day. In one review, the famous Catholic writer François Mauriac wrote: "We have literally reached the limits of the abject. This is the ipecac they made us swallow as children to induce vomiting."

The Second Sex remains controversial today, even among some feminists. But the book's place as a foundational text of twentieth-century feminism remains secure.

Simone de Beauvoir, photographed in 1959.

SEE ALSO *A Vindication of the Rights of Woman* (1792), Emergence of Feminist Philosophy (c. 1976)

1949

ECOCENTRISM

Aldo Leopold (1887–1948),
Arne Naess (1912–2009)

OVER THE PAST CENTURY OR SO, human attitudes toward nature and the environment have changed dramatically. Until recently, most people thought about nature in strongly human-centered terms. Nature was not viewed as having value in itself; it was something to be conquered and exploited purely for human benefit. These kinds of attitudes began to change in the 1960s when the modern environmental movement began. People then began to worry about the long-term costs of things like pollution and resource depletion to human welfare. This was an example of what the Norwegian philosopher Arne Naess terms "shallow ecology."

> Humans should not regard themselves as conquerors of the biotic community on earth, but rather as plain members and citizens of it.

Naess himself pleaded for a much more radical form of environmentalism called "deep ecology." Deep ecologists believe that all forms of life have value, and that humans have no right to harm other living things "except to satisfy vital needs." A view that comes somewhere in between shallow ecology and Naess's deep ecology is the ecocentric "land ethic" of Aldo Leopold. According to Leopold, humans should not regard themselves as conquerors of the biotic community on earth, but rather as plain members and citizens of it. Ethical concern should be shown not only to humans but to soils, waters, plants, animals as well—in short, to the land itself.

Leopold was born in Burlington, Iowa, and educated at Yale, where he received a master's degree in forestry. After working for the U.S. Forest Service for many years, Leopold taught game management at the University of Wisconsin. In 1935, he bought an abandoned farm in central Wisconsin and renovated a dilapidated chicken coop ("The Shack") for him and his family to live in on weekends. His great work, *A Sand County Almanac* (1949), is a lyrical expression of the joys Leopold found in the Wisconsin wilderness and in other beautiful parts of America.

Unlike supporters of animal rights, Leopold does not believe that our primary ethical concern should be with the health or welfare of individual plants or animals. Instead, we should be concerned with the good of ecological wholes, what he calls "the integrity, stability, and beauty" of entire ecosystems and species. This holistic approach to nature is now very popular in mainstream environmental theory and policy.

SEE ALSO The Moral Sense (1725), *Animal Liberation* (1975)

PHILOSOPHICAL INVESTIGATIONS

Ludwig Wittgenstein (1889–1951)

WITTGENSTEIN WAS BORN IN VIENNA, the son of an iron and steel magnate. Trained as an engineer, he became interested in the foundations of logic and mathematics after reading the works of Bertrand Russell and Gottlob Frege (1848–1925). After studying with Russell at Cambridge, Wittgenstein served in the Austrian army during World War I. He wrote his great early work, the *Tractatus Logico-Philosophicus* (1921), while serving on active duty. After the war, Wittgenstein worked as a gardener and schoolteacher before returning to Cambridge, where he taught philosophy for the rest of his life. His most important book, *Philosophical Investigations* (1953), was published two years after his death.

Philosophical Investigations regularly tops lists of the twentieth century's most important and influential philosophy books. Its claims about the connection between meaning and use, the incoherence of the notion of a private language, the notion of rule-following, the "family resemblances" that sometimes characterize various uses of a word, and philosophy as a form of therapy aimed at "dissolving" philosophical problems rather than solving them, all had a huge impact on mid- and late-twentieth-century philosophy. But perhaps Wittgenstein's most influential idea was that of the complexity of language and the importance of what he called "language-games."

In the *Tractatus*, Wittgenstein had defended a picture theory of meaning that saw language as having just one function: to state facts. In the *Investigations*, he recognized that this picture was far too simple. Language is a social practice, a "form of life," and therefore is as rich and multifaceted as human interaction itself. We use language not only to convey facts but also to pray, sing, tell jokes, give orders, ask questions, write poems, and so forth. Words are not simply name tags that we affix to things; they are more like tools in a toolbox that have a wide variety of purposes. A word like *if*, for example, does not name any object or refer to any fact; its meaning depends on context and use.

This is one reason why Wittgenstein compares language to games: to emphasize how meanings are context-dependent and arise only within a practice, just as individual rules about when a runner or batter is "out" make sense only within the context of the game of baseball as a whole. A second reason is to stress the rule-governed nature of language. What moves are allowed in chess is determined by rules, which in turn are grounded in social conventions. Likewise, Wittgenstein argues, what "moves" are allowed in language are determined by rules and conventions. Moreover, these rules and conventions vary from context to context. An expression like "stay off the grass" might mean one thing in a lawn-care seminar and quite another in a drug-counseling session. In short, the richness of language should never be forgotten.

> Language is a social practice, a "form of life," and therefore is as rich and multifaceted as human interaction itself.

SEE ALSO Postmodernism (1979)

SCIENTIFIC REVOLUTIONS

Thomas Kuhn (1922–96)

UNTIL RECENTLY, IT WAS WIDELY ASSUMED by historians and philosophers of science that science advances slowly through the gradual accumulation of new facts and information. This idea was challenged in Thomas Kuhn's landmark 1962 book, *The Structure of Scientific Revolutions*. According to Kuhn, the biggest scientific advances occur quickly, by

The Nicolaus Copernicus Monument in Warsaw, 1830,
by Danish sculptor Bertel Thorvaldsen.

means of sweeping scientific "revolutions." After more than half a century, Kuhn's book remains one of the most-cited and influential academic books of our time.

Kuhn was a physicist by training but switched to the history and philosophy of science while teaching at Harvard in the 1950s. Later he taught at Berkeley, Princeton, and the Massachusetts Institute of Technology.

When Kuhn studied big scientific changes like the Copernican revolution, he observed a common pattern. For long periods there would be little change, with most scientific work being a kind of puzzle solving within an accepted scientific theory, the reigning scientific "paradigm" as he called it. This is the period of what Kuhn dubbed "normal science." But then problems with the accepted paradigm begin to be noticed. Observations are made that conflict with the paradigm. At first these "anomalies" are swept under the rug or ad hoc modifications are made to the accepted theory to address the conflicts. Eventually, however, the anomalies become too severe and a "crisis" occurs in the scientific community. A new, competing paradigm is proposed. A battle occurs between advocates of the old and new paradigms. Neither side can produce knockdown arguments: the competing theories are "incommensurable," often there are no paradigm-neutral ways of assessing the relevant data, and it is always possible to save one's preferred paradigm by explaining away the apparent anomalies. Over time, the new paradigm prevails, not because of rationally conclusive evidence, but partly for sociological and psychological reasons that have nothing to do with the scientific data. A new period of normal science then begins, but whether the new paradigm is closer to "the truth" than the old one is a question science cannot answer.

Kuhn's book raises a host of troubling questions. Is science an objective way of knowing? Are all claims to scientific knowledge relative? Is science a more reliable way of knowing than (say) art, mysticism, or voodoo? Kuhn's work is at the center of these ongoing debates.

SEE ALSO The Birth of Modern Science (1543)

1966

SOUL-MAKING THEODICY

John Hick (1922–2012)

FOR MANY PEOPLE, the biggest obstacle to belief in God is the reality and pervasiveness of evil. If God is all-powerful and all-knowing, it seems that He must have the power and wisdom to prevent evil. And if He is perfectly good, it seems that He must have the desire to prevent evil. So why does evil exist?

For well over a thousand years, the standard Christian response to the problem of evil was rooted in the thought of St. Augustine. Augustine argued that all evil is either sin or the justified punishment for sin. God rightly permits sin because of the great value He places on free will. And He justifiably permits other forms of evil, such as natural disasters and the suffering of infants and animals, because these serve as just punishment for sin. Of course, babies and animals cannot themselves sin. But Augustine argues that they still deserve punishment because of the sin of Adam and Eve. Babies inherit the original sinfulness of Adam and Eve, and animals suffer because all of nature is "fallen" as a result of original sin.

> A better response to the problem of evil, Hick argued, is to see evil as a necessary condition for "soul-making."

In 1966, British philosopher of religion John Hick critiqued this traditional response to the problem of evil in an important book, *Evil and the God of Love*. Hick noted that modern science has shown that animals were suffering and dying long before there were any humans on earth. Thus, it cannot be claimed that all animal pain is due to the sin of Adam and Eve. Hick also argued that a truly loving and just God would not punish innocent babies for sins committed by one of their remote ancestors.

A better response to the problem of evil, Hick argued, is to see evil as a necessary condition for "soul-making." In this view, God allows evil because it provides opportunities for moral and spiritual growth. Only by wrestling with real hardships and challenges can we perfect our characters and become the type of person God wants us to be. Since most of us fall far short of perfection in this life, Hick argues that God must allow further opportunities for soul-making in the afterlife. Ultimately, he claims, everyone will be saved and evil will be just a memory.

SEE ALSO *Candide* (1759), Hume's *Dialogues* (1779)

DECONSTRUCTION

Jacques Derrida (1930–2004)

THOUGH JACQUES DERRIDA is unquestionably one of the most influential French philosophers of the latter half of the twentieth century, he continues to be largely ignored by Anglo-American analytic philosophers. Partly this is due to what John Passmore (d. 2004) has described as the "jungle-like obscurity" of Derrida's notoriously dense and unconventional prose. But another reason is that Derrida attacks the very enterprise of philosophy itself, at least as most Western philosophers have conceived of that project. If Derrida is right, philosophy is a good deal like literature and should give up its "logocentric" fixation on logic, rational arguments, and general theories.

Derrida was born near Algiers in French Algeria to a family of Sephardic Jews. After moving to Paris at age nineteen, he studied and later taught at the elite École normale supérieure. In 1967, Derrida rocketed to fame when he published three books that introduced and demonstrated the concept of deconstruction: *L'écriture et la différence* (*Writing and Difference*), *De la grammatologie* (*Of Grammatology*), and *La voix et le phénomène* (*Speech and Phenomena*).

Derrida presents deconstruction as both a method of reading texts and a way of criticizing intellectual systems. As a method of reading texts, deconstruction seeks to tease out internal problems that reveal hidden contradictions and alternative meanings. As a method of conceptual critique it is primarily a technique for "destabilizing" traditional "binary oppositions," such as reason/emotion, male/female, reality/appearance, objective/subjective, truth/fiction, and so forth. One way it does this is by showing that the features that supposedly characterize the "inferior" concept are also found in the "superior" alternative. Derrida's basic critique of traditional philosophy is that it has been too logocentric in its stress on logic, rationality, and the ability of reason to penetrate to a realm of truth that exists independently of human thought and language. Western thought, he claims, has been dominated by a "metaphysics of presence" that stresses direct knowing of eternal and unchanging realities. By contrast, Derrida believes that reality can best be understood in terms of difference, elusiveness, and the "deferment" of meaning (and therefore truth) that results from the dependency of meaning on the vast interconnected web of language.

As a method of reading texts, deconstruction seeks to tease out internal problems that reveal hidden contradictions and alternative meanings.

SEE ALSO Power/Knowledge (1975), Postmodernism (1979)

A THEORY OF JUSTICE

John Rawls (1921–2002)

JOHN RAWLS'S 1971 BOOK *A Theory of Justice* is widely considered the most important work of political philosophy in the twentieth century. Its importance lies not only in the power and sophistication of the theory it defends, but in its effects as well. *A Theory of Justice* revitalized the field of political philosophy, gave new vibrancy to political liberalism, reenergized the social-contract tradition of political theorizing, and dealt a severe blow to utilitarianism, long the most dominant ethical theory.

Rawls was born in Baltimore and received his PhD from Princeton. During World War II, he served as an infantryman and lost his faith in God after witnessing horrific scenes in the Pacific. He taught philosophy at Cornell and MIT for a number of years, publishing a number of important articles in ethics and political philosophy, before moving to Harvard in 1962. Following publication of his magnum opus, *A Theory of Justice*, in 1971, Rawls wrote a number of other important books, including *Political Liberalism* (1993) and *The Law of Peoples* (1999).

In *A Theory of Justice*, Rawls defends a liberal theory of justice he calls "justice as fairness." The basic idea is that a just society should be governed by principles of justice that would be chosen in a discussion format that was fair. Rawls calls such a format the "original position." This is a situation in which the participants know general facts about economics and human nature but otherwise operate under a "veil of ignorance" about the specifics of their own society, social status in that society, and their own life goals. The purpose of this veil of ignorance is to make sure that nobody can skew the discussion to their own advantage. Under these conditions, Rawls argues, social contractors in the original position would choose two basic principles of justice. One ensures equal basic liberties; the other prohibits social and economic inequalities, except when such inequalities benefit everyone in society. The upshot is a liberal regime in which freedom and equality are the two most important political values.

Rawls's theory of justice has been criticized on many fronts. But his work is widely hailed for the power of its central idea and the brilliance and depth of its elaboration.

In *A Theory of Justice*, John Rawls describes "justice as fairness" as the idea that a just society should be governed by principles of justice that would be chosen in a discussion format that was fair. Here, an 1882 engraving featuring the personification of justice—Lady Justice, holding her scales.

SEE ALSO Human Rights (1689), *The Social Contract* (1762), Political Libertarianism (1974)

POLITICAL LIBERTARIANISM

Robert Nozick (1938–2002)

THE TWENTIETH CENTURY PRODUCED two great classics of analytic political philosophy. One was John Rawls's *A Theory of Justice* (1971). The other was *Anarchy, State, and Utopia*, published three years later by Rawls's Harvard colleague Robert Nozick. The books argued for radically different conclusions. Whereas Rawls defended an egalitarian liberal welfare state, Nozick supported a minimal "night-watchman" government limited to the narrow functions of protection against force, fraud, theft, and other violations of individual rights.

> Nozick argues that taxing one person to benefit another is a form of forced labor that wrongly treats persons as mere means to desired ends.

Nozick was born in Brooklyn, the son of Russian immigrant Jews. After graduating from Columbia, he received a PhD in philosophy from Princeton, where he became a convinced libertarian, largely through reading the works of economists Murray Rothbard (1926–95) and Friedrich Hayek (1899–1992). In 1969, Nozick moved from Rockefeller University to Harvard, where he taught for the rest of his career.

Like Kant, Nozick believed that humans must be treated as

autonomous "ends in themselves." In virtue of this inherent dignity, people possess a host of robust natural rights. Among these are a right of self-ownership that, among other things, makes it wrong for government to redistribute income. In *Anarchy, State, and Utopia*, Nozick argues that taxing one person to benefit another is a form of forced labor that wrongly treats persons as mere means to desired ends. A just and morally defensible state would respect individual rights and embrace an "entitlement" approach to wealth distribution that views all holdings as just, as long as they arose from a just situation by just steps.

Anarchy, State, and Utopia, which won a National Book Award in 1975, was notable not only for its defense of libertarianism and critique of Rawls, but also for its powerful attacks on utilitarian ethics. In critiquing utilitarianism, Nozick created a famous thought experiment known as the "experience machine." Suppose you could plug into a virtual-reality machine that would give you any experience you desired. Should you plug in for life, knowing that you will thereby be guaranteed a lifetime of pleasurable experiences? According to classical utilitarianism, such experiences are the only things that ultimately matter in life. The fact that most people would choose not to plug into the experience machine seems to show that this intuition is not widely shared.

SEE ALSO Human Rights (1689), *A Theory of Justice* (1971)

"WHAT IS IT LIKE TO BE A BAT?"

Thomas Nagel (b. 1937)

THOMAS NAGEL IS A LEADING AMERICAN PHILOSOPHER who has made major contributions to many areas of philosophy, including philosophy of mind, ethics, and political philosophy. Throughout his career, Nagel has focused on the contrast between objective and subjective points

An engraving of western barbastelle bats, 1897. Nagel uses the example of consciousness in bats to criticize purely physicalistic theories of mind. He writes that "in contemplating the [exact nature of] bats we are in much the same position that intelligent bats or Martians would occupy if they tried to form a conception of what it was like to be us."

of view, arguing that objective forms of knowing are not always better for finite creatures like ourselves. Nagel is also well known for his critique of reductionistic theories of mind. His 1974 article "What Is It Like to Be a Bat?" is a classic attack on attempts to treat the mind as a purely physical phenomenon.

Nagel was born in Belgrade, in present-day Serbia. After obtaining a PhD from Harvard in 1963, he taught at Berkeley and Princeton before moving to New York University in 1980. Among his many important books are *The Possibility of Altruism* (1970), *Mortal Questions* (1979), *The View from Nowhere* (1986), and *Mind and Cosmos* (2012).

In "What Is It Like to Be a Bat?" Nagel uses the example of consciousness in bats to criticize purely physicalistic theories of mind. Bats use echolocating sonar to catch flying insects at night. Nagel argues that it is likely that bats, which are mammals, have some form of conscious awareness, but that we have no clue what their inner experiences are like. Science can tell us a great deal about how bats' sonar works, but it cannot give us any real insight into "what it is like to be a bat"—what a bat senses, for example, when it detects a flying moth in its perceptual field. More generally, Nagel claims, theories of mind that try to reduce mental experiences to neurochemical events in the brain miss out on the whole blooming, buzzing *qualitative* dimension of consciousness. The way things feel and seem—the smell of fresh-cut grass, the taste of a strawberry, the redness of a rose—is simply left out of reductionistic accounts of the mind. This is what reduction-minded neuroscientists call the "hard problem of consciousness." It was Nagel who gave canonical expression to the problem.

SEE ALSO Philosophical Zombies (1991)

ANIMAL LIBERATION

Peter Singer (b. 1946)

DURING THE 1960S AND 1970S, many people began to rethink traditional attitudes toward women, minorities, gays, and the environment. As part of this cultural shift, there was a new focus on how humans treat animals. This marked the beginning of what is commonly called the "animal rights movement." At the forefront of this movement was a young Australian philosopher named Peter Singer.

Singer first achieved prominence as a defender of animal welfare when he published a long book review titled "Animal Liberation" in the *New York Review of Books* in April 1973. Two years later, he published a book, also titled *Animal Liberation*, which is often called the "Bible of the animal rights movement."

Describing Singer as an advocate of "animal rights" is misleading, however, because his defense of animals is purely utilitarian. His claim is not that animals have fundamental moral rights but that they have "interests" that must be respected. Like humans, higher animals like cows and pigs have an interest in avoiding pain and suffering. Ethics requires that we treat equal interests equally. Thus, it is wrong to care about human pain but to ignore or discount animal pain. To do so is a form of unjustifiable discrimination that Singer (borrowing a term coined by Richard Ryder [b. 1940]) calls "speciesism." The upshot is that we should stop raising animals for food; abolish hunting, trapping, and zoos; drastically curtail animal experimentation; and become vegetarians.

Singer's book helped to galvanize the nascent animal rights movement. When *Animal Liberation* was first published, very few people in Western societies believed that eating animals was an ethical issue at all. A 2018 study estimates that roughly 5 percent of Americans are vegetarians, most for moral reasons, and the plant-based diet movement continues to grow.

As the animal rights movement has grown, defenders of animal welfare have generally moved away from the types of utilitarian arguments offered by Singer. Today animal rights are more commonly defended by invoking concepts like "intrinsic value," "reverence for life," "equal inherent worth," or other such deontological notions. Such dignity-based arguments are widely thought to provide a firmer grounding for rights than Singer's utilitarianism does.

A contemporary photograph of a cattle-feeding trough on a farm in Saskatchewan, Canada.

SEE ALSO The Moral Sense (1725), Utilitarianism (1789), Refined Utilitarianism (1863), Ecocentrism (1949)

POWER/KNOWLEDGE

Michel Foucault (1926–1984)

Portrait of Michel Foucault, 1979.

MANY STRANDS OF RECENT FRENCH PHILOSOPHY have denied the possibility of objective knowledge and embraced some version or another of relativism. Various labels are used to describe such schools of thought, including post-structuralism, deconstructionism, and postmodernism. One important French thinker who is often classified as a post-structuralist is Michel Foucault. In a series of notable books beginning in the early 1960s, Foucault explored what he termed the "archeology" and "genealogy" of knowledge. Both methods deny the possibility of objective knowledge or universal reason.

Foucault was born in Poitiers and educated in the École normale supérieure, the elite Parisian school that, since its founding in 1794, has produced many leading French philosophers. Early in his career, Foucault embraced Marxism and phenomenological existentialism, but in the 1960s he developed an approach to intellectual history he called the "archeology of knowledge." In works such as *The History of Madness* (1961), *The Order of Things* (1966), and *The Archeology of Knowledge* (1969), Foucault argued that there are no standards of truth or falsity that apply outside "discursive practices," that is, particular culturally conditioned conceptual frameworks of language and thought. These frameworks, he claimed, are governed by rules, some of which are unconscious, that set limits to what is thinkable in a particular system. The task of archeology of knowledge is to show how claims that purport to be based on objective knowledge, scientific fact, and universal truths are really relative and contingent.

Foucault later extended his archeological approach to include a theory of how systems of thought change over time, which he called the "genealogy of knowledge." From 1975 until his AIDS-related death in 1984, Foucault wrote a series of books that sought to show the fundamental connection between power and knowledge. Claims of objective and universal truth, he argued, are used to mask systems of control. By recognizing that what is presented as "human nature" or "self-evident truth" or "scientific fact" is actually a contingent product of historically conditioned forces, individuals are liberated to pursue their own freely chosen experiments in living.

SEE ALSO Deconstruction (1967), Postmodernism (1979)

c. 1976

EMERGENCE OF FEMINIST PHILOSOPHY

Alison Jaggar (b. 1942),
Marilyn Frye (b. 1941), Jane English (b. 1942),
Sandra Harding (b. 1935), Carol C. Gould (n.d.),
and Marx Wartofsky (1928–97)

FEMINIST PHILOSOPHY IS IMPORTANT both for what it has done and for what it may yet achieve. Since its emergence in the mid-1970s, feminist philosophy has profoundly affected mainstream philosophical thought about issues of equality, social justice, patriarchy, gender, and identity. It has also posed deep challenges to long-held notions of objectivity, universality, rationality, dualistic thinking, essentialism, the public-private distinction, and the self, which continue to be hotly debated. Only the future will tell how these issues will play out.

The history of women in philosophy has not been a happy one. Until recently, women were largely excluded from philosophy because of patriarchal biases and traditional views of gender roles. Moreover, many of the great Western philosophers from ancient Greece to the modern era—including Aristotle, Aquinas, Rousseau, Kant, and Nietzsche—held deeply sexist views about women. Important forerunners of modern feminism such as Mary Wollstonecraft, John Stuart Mill, Harriet Taylor, and Simone de Beauvoir challenged long-held assumptions about women's inferiority and women's roles in society. Feminist philosophy emerged in the 1970s as an outgrowth of the women's movement of the 1960s; among the early pioneers were Alison Jaggar, Marilyn Frye, Jane English, and Sandra Harding. Carol C. Gould and Marx Wartofsky published the first anthology of feminist philosophy, titled *Women and Philosophy: Toward a Theory of Liberation*, in 1976.

Feminist philosophy is highly diverse; those who practice it may embrace liberalism, socialism, Marxism, pragmatism, postmodernism, or any number of other isms. What unites feminist philosophers is a shared conviction that relations between the sexes are unequal, oppressive, and unjust; that it is important to identify and remedy the sources of women's subordination; and that traditional philosophy has been male-biased in a variety of ways. Many strands of feminist philosophy deny the possibility of objective knowledge or universal truths. Others claim that reason and emotion are coequal sources of knowledge. Some feminists reject all forms of hierarchical thinking, including any human superiority over nature. Still others deny that rules or principles should play a significant role in moral decision-making. Such claims pose radical challenges not only to traditional philosophy, but also to science and many aspects of contemporary culture. For this reason, among others, feminist philosophy is one of the most important and exciting movements in contemporary philosophy.

> Until recently, women were largely excluded from philosophy because of patriarchal biases and traditional views of gender roles.

SEE ALSO *A Vindication of the Rights of Woman* (1792), *The Second Sex* (1949)

MORAL ANTI-REALISM

John Leslie Mackie (1917–81)

ROUGHLY, MORAL ANTI-REALISM is the view that there are no moral facts or moral values, or at least none that are mind-independent. Prominent moral antirealists include Protagoras, who defended moral relativism; David Hume, who claimed that moral values are "projected" onto objects that do not in fact possess them; A. J. Ayer, who defended a version of emotivism; and Friedrich Nietzsche, who denied that there are any moral facts and claimed that all ethical truth claims are merely "perspectival." In 1977, the prominent Australian philosopher J. L. Mackie published an influential defense of moral anti-realism in *Ethics: Inventing Right and Wrong*.

> If objective moral properties existed, [Mackie] argues, they'd be very strange and mysterious sorts of entities.

Unlike moral noncognitivists such as Ayer, who claimed that moral statements are purely emotive and do not even purport to be true, Mackie concedes that when people say things like "Hitler was evil" (my example, not his) they are asserting something that they believe to be true. The problem, he argues, is that there are no moral facts or moral truths, so we must embrace an "error theory" of moral language. In other words, when people say things like "Hitler was evil," they are implicitly asserting that "Hitler was really and objectively evil," which is false, because there are no objective moral facts or objective moral truths. Most moral talk, Mackie claims, is bunk, much as talk about the Loch Ness monster is bunk.

He gives a number of arguments to support this theory. The most important is what he calls the "argument from queerness." If objective moral properties existed, he argues, they'd be very strange and mysterious sorts of entities—nonmaterial entities that somehow "supervene" on material features of the world but aren't reducible to those features. Moreover, how could we be aware of these entities without possessing some special faculty of moral perception or intuition, which fits poorly with a modern scientific worldview? For such reasons, Mackie embraces a view that he calls "moral skepticism": there are no objective moral facts, even though most people mistakenly assume that there are.

Mackie's vigorous, clearly written defense of his error theory of moral talk sparked a renewed interest in moral anti-realism. According to a recent survey, only a slight majority of professional philosophers accept or lean toward moral realism. Mackie's book may well have contributed to this shift away from realist views of ethics.

SEE ALSO Protagoras and Relativism (c. 450 BCE), Morality Is Rooted in Feeling (1751), Logical Positivism (1936)

POSTMODERNISM

Jean-François Lyotard (1924–98)

POSTMODERNISM IS NOTORIOUSLY DIFFICULT TO DEFINE. Versions of postmodernist thought are found in film, architecture, literature, the visual arts, and music. As a philosophical movement, postmodernism can be broadly characterized as a family of theories that rejects core elements of Enlightenment "modernism," such as objective knowledge, human progress by means of science and technology, foundational beliefs that are 100 percent certain, language as an accurate "mirror of nature," and faith in our ability to construct general theories that can provide comprehensive explanations of nature and society. Leading thinkers who are often classified as postmodernists include twentieth-century French philosophers Michel Foucault, Jacques Derrida, Jean Baudrillard, Gilles Deleuze, and Jean-François Lyotard. It was Lyotard who first popularized the term "postmodernism" in his important book *The Postmodern Condition: A Report on Knowledge* (1979).

Lyotard was born outside of Paris to middle-class parents. As a young secondary-school teacher, Lyotard became radicalized and spent fifteen years working for far-left revolutionary causes. After receiving his doctorate in his mid-thirties, he taught at the University of Paris, Vincennes, and at other universities in France and abroad. Publication of *The Postmodern Condition* brought him international prominence.

In *The Postmodern Condition*, Lyotard famously defines postmodernism as "incredulity towards metanarratives." What he means is that educated people today have generally become distrustful of grand, catchall theories like Marxism, or the perfectibility of humanity through scientific progress that appeal to supposed "universal truths" and promise some glorious, not-yet-realized lollapalooza. Such distrust is healthy, Lyotard argues, because grand theories tend to ignore the messy heterogeneity of reality and the importance of individual events, and are often used to prop up some power elite. Like most postmodernists, Lyotard favors replacing big metanarratives with more modest "localized" narratives that recognize a variety of legitimate standpoints. One metanarrative that he criticizes at length is that of science as a privileged form of "objective" knowing that will inevitably lead to human enlightenment and emancipation. Drawing from Wittgenstein's later philosophy, Lyotard argues that science is simply one "language game" among many, and that no language game can claim that it alone is legitimate.

Jean-François Lyotard in Hannover, Germany, in 1992.

SEE ALSO *Philosophical Investigations* (1953), Deconstruction (1967), Power/ Knowledge (1975)

THE CHINESE ROOM

John Searle (b. 1932)

ONE OF THE MOST DISCUSSED ARGUMENTS in recent philosophy is John Searle's intriguing thought experiment known as the "Chinese Room." If Searle is right, no matter how sophisticated computers eventually become, no computer could ever actually think.

Searle was born in Denver, studied at the University of Wisconsin-Madison, and received his doctorate from Oxford. He recently retired from the University of California, Berkeley, where he had taught since 1959. Among his many important books are *Speech Acts* (1969), *Intentionality* (1983), and *The Mystery of Consciousness* (1997). Searle is a leading critic of materialistic theories of the mind that deny the existence of nonreducible mental events. He views mind as an emergent nonphysical product of the physical brain. In 1980, Searle published a famous article, "Mind, Brains, and Programs," in the journal *Behavioral and Brain Sciences*. It used the idea of an unwitting question-and-answer process—the "Chinese Room" thought experiment—to challenge mainstream views about whether machines could ever be conscious or think. Here's how it works:

Imagine that you're a native English speaker who speaks no Chinese. You're locked in a room with two slits, a big book of instructions, a pen, and some scratch paper. Slips of paper with mysterious marks on them fall in through one slit. You use the book of instructions to match these marks with other marks that you write down on the scratch paper, and then you push the paper out through the other slit. Later you find out that the slips of paper contained questions written in Chinese, and that what you wrote down on the scratch paper were witty and highly appropriate answers in Chinese. So good, in fact, were your answers that you fooled everybody into thinking that the answers came from a real Chinese-speaking human being.

What does this show about the possibility of artificial intelligence?

According to Searle, it shows that no computer could ever think. What you did is exactly what a digital computer does: use formal rules to manipulate symbols to produce outputs. You had no understanding at all of what the string of marks you received or sent meant. Likewise, he argues, a computer could conceivably mimic human intelligence, but it could never be conscious or engage in genuine thinking.

The "Chinese Room" thought experiment [challenged] mainstream views about whether machines could ever be conscious or think.

SEE ALSO Hume's *Dialogues* (1779)

THE REVIVAL
OF VIRTUE ETHICS

Elizabeth Anscombe (1919–2001),
Alasdair MacIntyre (b. 1929)

From Aristotle until roughly 1600, the dominant approach to ethics in Western civilization was what we today call "virtue ethics." According to virtue ethics, the central focus of moral theory and reflection should be on questions of character, virtue, and wisdom—not on identifying and following correct moral rules or on maximizing good consequences.

> According to virtue ethics, the central focus of moral theory and reflection should be on questions of character, virtue, and wisdom.

Broadly, virtue ethicists focus mainly on two questions: (1) What does it mean to be a really good person? and (2) What virtues, or excellences of mind and character, are needed to become such a person? Aristotle was a virtue ethicist in this sense, as were Thomas Aquinas and most other medieval philosophers. In modern philosophy, this way of approaching ethics largely broke down. Instead, philosophers such as Immanuel Kant and John Stuart Mill believed that the central task of ethics was that of working out a good ethical decision procedure—a method for deciding what is morally right or wrong, or good or bad, in pretty much every conceivable situation. It wasn't until the latter half of the twentieth century that thinkers such as Elizabeth Anscombe and Alasdair MacIntyre made a serious case for reviving virtue ethics.

Anscombe, a Catholic philosopher born in Limerick, Ireland, was much influenced by Wittgenstein. In 1958, she published a now-classic article titled "Modern Moral Philosophy." In that paper she argues that modern ethical theory and discourse are rudderless and incoherent, because they employed terms like "obligation" and "ought" that were based on an older, Judeo-Christian way of thinking about ethics that has largely been abandoned. In her opinion, philosophers should stop doing ethics until an adequate psychological basis has been found for doing ethics productively.

An even more influential stimulus for the revival of virtue ethics was Alasdair MacIntyre's 1981 book, *After Virtue*. MacIntyre, a Scottish philosopher, offers a detailed historical account of how modern ethics fell into disarray and proposes a cure that sought to ground ethics in communities and traditions of virtue. In later books, he argues that the tradition of virtue theory rooted in the thoughts of Aristotle and Aquinas—but modernized in certain ways—offers the best available approach to ethics today.

SEE ALSO *Nicomachean Ethics* (c. 330 BCE), Natural Law (c. 1270)

IN A DIFFERENT VOICE

Carol Gilligan (b. 1936)

A PROMINENT THEME in some strands of recent feminist thought has been that women tend to approach ethics differently than men. Women, it is claimed, tend to value relationships and connections—an "ethic of care"—whereas men tend to value rights, autonomy, and impartiality—an

Carol Gilligan photographed at the University of Cambridge, where she was Pitt Professor of American History and Institutions, April 1994.

"ethic of justice." The origins of this important contemporary debate can largely be traced to the pathbreaking work of Carol Gilligan.

Gilligan, who now teaches at New York University, taught for many years at Harvard, where she received her PhD in Social Psychology. At Harvard, Gilligan worked as a research assistant to Lawrence Kohlberg (1927–87), creator of a highly influential theory of moral development. She was struck by the fact that women tended to score lower on Kohlberg's moral reasoning scale than men did. Noting that all of his original test subjects were males, Gilligan wondered if Kohlberg's methodology might be male-biased. When Gilligan conducted her own interviews with both women and men, she began to hear "a different voice" in the way they tended to wrestle with moral issues. Her resulting book, *In a Different Voice: Psychological Theory and Women's Development* (1982), has generated major discussion in both psychology and ethics.

Building on Gilligan's work, a number of feminist ethicists have defended versions of an ethic of care. Theorists such as Nel Noddings (b. 1929) have argued that traditional ethics has overemphasized values such as objectivity, impartiality, individual rights, autonomy, and rule-driven decision making, while giving short shrift to values such as care, compassion, love, friendship, and relatedness. While acknowledging the importance of rights, rules, and other core notions of traditional ethics, these theorists argue that an ethic of care is generally superior to an ethic of justice and would lead to a more caring and less violent world. Questions abound about Gilligan's work and its implications for ethics and psychology. How strong is the evidence that men and women differ in the way they tend to think about moral issues? Might an ethic of care reinforce stereotypes about caregiving being primarily women's responsibility and lead some women to neglect their own health and happiness? Can a viable ethic of care be defended? These are all important ongoing debates.

SEE ALSO *A Vindication of the Rights of Woman* (1792), *The Second Sex* (1949), Emergence of Feminist Philosophy (c. 1976)

REVIVAL OF CHRISTIAN PHILOSOPHY

Alvin Plantinga (b. 1932)

FOR MANY CENTURIES, great thinkers in Christian Europe, such as St. Augustine and Aquinas, practiced a form of what is now called Christian philosophy. In this view, faith and reason were seen as allies, rather than as strangers or enemies. Since all truth flows from God, it was assumed that reason and revelation must harmonize. This did not mean that philosophy collapses into theology; they each have their proper spheres. The idea was that philosophy could be done better if it was guided and illumined by divinely revealed truth.

This way of doing philosophy was widely rejected in the modern era. A complete separation of philosophy and theology was believed to be necessary to avoid theological feuds and to appeal to reasonable people of all creeds, including religious skeptics. In the 1970s and 1980s, a significant revival of Christian philosophy occurred. The central figure in that revival was the distinguished American philosopher Alvin Plantinga, who taught for most of his career at the University of Notre Dame. In 1984, Plantinga published an article titled "Advice to Christian Philosophers," which became something of a manifesto for an unabashed contemporary form of Christian philosophy.

Plantinga argued that Christian philosophers should see themselves as part of the Christian community, with an important role to play in building up that community. Specifically, they should use their talents and specialized training to refute attacks on the Christian faith; to offer reasoned arguments in support of Christian belief; to clarify, systematize, and deepen central Christian teachings; and to explore the implications of Christian theism for the whole range of questions philosophers address. Too often,

Plantinga suggested, Christian philosophers kowtow to current fashions in philosophy, most of which are hostile to Christian theism. To serve the Christian community better, they should display more independence, more integrity, and more courage and self-confidence.

Plantinga's call to arms received a hearty response. Hundreds of young Christian intellectuals flocked to universities like Notre Dame and Baylor that offered strong doctoral programs in Christian philosophy. Today Christian philosophy is flourishing in a way that has not been seen for many centuries.

This mosaic mural by American artist Millard Sheets, *The Word of Life*, adorns the facade of the Hesburgh Library at the University of Notre Dame, a Catholic research university in South Bend, Indiana. The mural, which faces the football stadium, is nicknamed Touchdown Jesus.

SEE ALSO Augustine's Conversion (386), The Five Ways (c. 1265), Natural Law (c. 1270), The New Atheists (2004)

RELIGIOUS PLURALISM

John Hick (1922–2012)

MANY RELIGIOUS BELIEVERS TODAY are inclined to accept some form of religious pluralism—the view, roughly, that many religions are true or offer equally effective pathways to salvation. There are several different versions of religious pluralism, ranging from extreme pluralism, the view that all religions are equally true, to inclusive pluralism, the claim that all the great religions of the world provide authentic avenues for experiencing the divine and are more or less equally efficacious in producing salvific moral and spiritual transformation. The most prominent defender of religious pluralism is the distinguished British philosopher of religion John Hick.

In Hick's much-discussed 1989 book, *An Interpretation of Religion: Human Responses to the Transcendent*, he defends a version of inclusive pluralism that owes much to Immanuel Kant. Hick believes that there is a divine Ultimate Reality (he calls it the "Real"), but that we can know practically nothing about it. Like Kant's noumenal reality, the Real is "ineffable"— beyond our human powers to describe or to conceptualize. Nevertheless, Hick argues, we can have authentic religious experiences of the Real. The problem is that all such experiences are filtered through different culturally shaped "lenses." Christians and Muslims, for example, experience God as a personal being, whereas Zen Buddhists and Hindu Advaita Vedantists experience it as an impersonal Absolute.

Hick suggests that all religious doctrines and language should be seen as faltering human attempts to describe the indescribable. What is important, Hick says, is that all major religions are in touch with the same divine Ultimate Reality (and are "equally true" in that sense), and that all major religions seem to be equally effective in what Hick sees as the basic goal of religion: the "transformation of human existence from self-centeredness to Reality-centeredness."

Hick's view is attractive to many supporters of religious pluralism, but it also raises problems. Mainstream theists of course reject out of hand the notion that statements like "God loves us" and "God is holy" are only "metaphorically true." And is it even possible to *be* (say) a Christian—or to obtain the spiritual fruits of being a Christian—if you believe that statements of core Christian belief like "Jesus saves" or "Jesus loves us" are literally false?

> What is important, Hick says, is that all major religions are in touch with the same divine Ultimate Reality.

SEE ALSO *Critique of Pure Reason* (1781), Soul-Making Theodicy (1966)

PHILOSOPHICAL ZOMBIES

Daniel Dennett (b. 1942)

ONE OF THE LIVELIEST, most interesting, and most widely read philosophers writing today is Daniel Dennett. As a philosopher, Dennett has done important work on free will, evolution, and the relation between science and religion, but his most notable contributions have been in the field of philosophy of mind. In his important 1991 book, *Consciousness Explained*, Dennett offers a materialistic theory of the mind that tries to break free of a host of traditional views that he believes have impeded a scientific understanding of consciousness. Among these obstructive views is that so-called "philosophical zombies" could exist.

Dennett was born in Boston and educated at Harvard and Oxford University. Since 1971, he has taught at Tufts University, where he codirects the Center for Cognitive Studies. He is the author of over a dozen books and more than four hundred scholarly articles.

> Dennett claims that such beings are not truly conceivable once we take the effort to imagine specific behaviors in detail.

In *Consciousness Explained*, Dennett seeks to undermine a traditional picture of the mind that he labels the "Cartesian theater." In this scenario, the mind is like a small movie theater where a homunculus, or tiny person, sits in a kind of control room watching sensory information projected on a screen and makes decisions that determine both thoughts and bodily behavior. In opposition to this, Dennett defends a "multiple drafts" view of consciousness, which conceives thoughts on an information-processing model as the product of "parallel, multitrack processes of interpretation and elaboration of sensory inputs"—a view that fits better, he thinks, with contemporary neuroscience and a thoroughly materialistic view of the mind.

In defending this view, Dennett weighs in on one of the more interesting thought experiments in contemporary philosophy: whether there could be creatures that are exactly like human beings in all physical respects but totally lack consciousness. These strange fictional creatures are known as "philosophical zombies," or "p-zombies" for short. Dennett claims that such beings are not truly conceivable once we take the effort to imagine specific behaviors in detail. Those who think they can conceive such creatures have not imagined thoroughly enough and "end up imagining something that violates their own definition," either by conceding physical differences or by allowing what amounts to states of consciousness. Happily, the great zombie debate still rages on today.

SEE ALSO Phenomenology (1900), "What Is It Like to Be a Bat?" (1974), The New Atheists (2004)

THE CAPABILITY APPROACH

Martha C. Nussbaum (b. 1947)

HOW SHOULD ONE MEASURE HUMAN WELFARE and international development? The traditional approach has been to look at purely quantitative measures such as per capita gross domestic product. Yet if a nation's GDP goes up while growing numbers of its citizens struggle to get an education, find work, or be treated with dignity, is the nation really better off? An influential new theory of social justice, well-being, and human development is known as the "capability approach" or the "human development approach." Among its primary architects is the American philosopher and classicist Martha Nussbaum, one of America's best-known public intellectuals.

A photograph of Martha Nussbaum by Robin Holland, 2008.

Born in New York City and raised in what she describes as an "East Coast WASP elite family" (she converted to Judaism in the early 1970s), Nussbaum received her PhD in philosophy from Harvard. Since 1994, Nussbaum has taught at the University of Chicago, where she is Ernst Freund Distinguished Service Professor of Law and Ethics, with joint appointments in the law school and the philosophy department. Her first major book, *The Fragility of Goodness: Luck and Ethics in Greek Tragedy and Philosophy* (1986), won wide acclaim throughout the humanities. A prolific writer, she has published widely on topics such as global ethics, feminism, multiculturalism, emotions, civil liberties, and the value of the liberal arts.

Nussbaum is perhaps best known, however, for her work in developing and popularizing the capability approach, which she lays out most fully in *Women and Human Development: The Capabilities Approach* (2000) and *Creating Capabilities: The Human Development Approach* (2011). First developed by the distinguished Indian philosopher and economist Amartya Sen (b. 1933), the capability approach is a broad theoretical framework for assessing human well-being and international development. The core tenet of the capability approach is that well-being should not be measured simply in terms of aggregate material resources or simple subjective criteria such as happiness, but rather by reference to multidimensional standards of human dignity and human flourishing that focus crucially on questions of what actual opportunities are available to people, of what they can really do and be. This is an approach that is increasingly gaining prominence in international development, scholarship, and policy-making.

SEE ALSO *A Theory of Justice* (1971)

THE NEW ATHEISTS

Richard Dawkins (b. 1941), Sam Harris (b. 1967),
Christopher Hitchens (1949–2011), Daniel Dennett (b. 1942),
Victor J. Stenger (1935–2014)

NEW ATHEISM IS A CONTEMPORARY ANTIRELIGIOUS, intellectual movement that erupted in the aftermath of the September 11, 2001, terrorist attacks in the United States. Its best-known defenders are Richard Dawkins, Sam Harris, Christopher Hitchens, Daniel Dennett, and Victor J. Stenger. While many critics claim that New Atheism often lacks the intellectual punching power of notable "old atheists," such as David Hume, John Stuart Mill, Bertrand Russell, and J. L. Mackie, it arguably has had a greater impact on public consciousness. Several books by the New Atheists, including Dawkins's *The God Delusion* (2006), were international best sellers.

As a movement, New Atheism is marked by a number of common themes. Generally, New Atheists reject the existence of the supernatural; are sharply critical of religion in all forms; see "faith" as an inherently irrational intellectual stance; are strongly pro-science; are committed to explaining religious belief in terms of biological evolution; and believe that objective, rationally defensible secular moral standards exist. New Atheism provoked a number of critical responses from leading theologians and philosophers of religion, including Alister McGrath, Keith Ward, William Lane Craig, and John F. Haught. Common criticisms were that the New Atheists often attacked traditionalist versions of religion; exaggerated the harms of religion while ignoring the benefits; misunderstood modern understandings of "faith"; knew little of contemporary theology; and relied on a form of "scientism" (the view that science is the only reliable way of knowing) that is indefensible and ultimately self-refuting.

Given the wide readership of the New Atheists, it's clear that they've struck a nerve. Certainly one of the worldwide megatrends of the past century has been the rapid growth of secularism. Religious belief has declined sharply in Europe, China, Canada, Australia, Israel, and other nations. The United States has long bucked this trend, though recent polls show that the number of religiously nonaffiliated "nones" is steadily rising. Certainly philosophers have become an increasingly skeptical bunch in recent decades. A 2013 survey by the website PhilPapers found that 62 percent of philosophers are atheists. What this bodes for the future is a fascinating question.

Richard Dawkins speaks about *The God Delusion*, his 2006 book, at a Barnes & Noble in New York City, March 14, 2008.

SEE ALSO Hume's *Dialogues* (1779), "God Is Dead" (1882), Atheistic Existentialism (1946)

COSMOPOLITANISM

Kwame Anthony Appiah (b. 1954)

LIKE ELEPHANTS AND WOLVES, humans are social animals. We like to run in packs, and often our strongest bonds and allegiances are to relatively small groups of family, friends, or tribe. Cultivating strong ties and

Kwame Anthony Appiah poses for a photograph in November 2007.

partialities to what sociologists call "in-group" associations can make for strong families, communities, and nations, and also provide individuals with a comforting sense of place and belonging. But as recent history demonstrates, it can also separate us into competing and mutually suspicious enclaves of "us" and "them." What's the right balance here in a globalized and increasingly interconnected world? One ancient but now increasingly popular approach is called "cosmopolitanism," and its best-known advocate is the London-born philosopher Kwame Anthony Appiah.

Appiah grew up in Ghana, the son of a white mother and a black father, both from distinguished political families. After receiving his doctorate from Cambridge University, Appiah taught at a number of leading American universities, including Harvard and Princeton. Recipient of the National Humanities Medal, he is currently a professor of philosophy and law at New York University.

In his 2006 book, *Cosmopolitanism: Ethics in a World of Strangers*, Appiah seeks to revive and refine the ancient Cynic and Stoic idea of being a *kosmopolitês* (citizen of the world). He argues that in a world in which strangers in distant lands can impact each other—for good or ill, in a myriad of ways—traditional views of ethics and politics must be rethought. We must, he claims, move beyond local ties and affiliations and recognize that in important respects, all human beings are citizens of a single global community. Some cosmopolitans advocate radical solutions such as a rejection of patriotism or the establishment of a single world state. Appiah argues for a more moderate form of cosmopolitanism that centers on two central values: universal concern and respect for legitimate difference. In brief, he maintains, we need to recognize that we do have obligations to others— even strangers—in virtue of our shared humanity, and we must develop habits of coexistence, mutual respect, and genuine conversation across cultural boundaries.

SEE ALSO Cynicism (c. 400 BCE)

2016

THE GOOD PLACE

William Irwin (b. 1970), Michael Schur (b. 1975)

PHILOSOPHY HAS LONG HAD A PUBLIC RELATIONS PROBLEM, particularly in the United States. In Europe, Asia, and some other parts of the world, philosophy books frequently appear on best-seller lists and philosophers are often respected public intellectuals. In America, by contrast, philosophy has long been seen as arcane, impractical, and remote from the problems of real life. Thankfully, this has started to change. One factor in this shift has been the contemporary philosophy and popular culture movement. Founded by philosopher William Irwin (b. 1970), the philosophy and popular culture movement seeks to use pop culture as a hook to inspire a love of philosophy and to demonstrate its relevance to everyday issues and problems. Over the past two decades, philosophers have applied their methods and insights to Harry Potter, *The Lord of the Rings*, *The Simpsons*, Batman, and many other pop culture topics.

In 2016, NBC jumped on this bandwagon with a new sitcom created by producer Michael Schur, *The Good Place*, which aired for four seasons and won numerous critical accolades. Set in the afterlife, *The Good Place* is the story of a self-absorbed woman, an indecisive ethics professor, and their two oddly matched friends who (spoiler alert!) manage to move from a hell-like Bad Place to a heaven-like Good Place, saving the human race along the way. Throughout the series, iconic philosophers such as Aristotle, Kant, Kierkegaard, and Nietzsche are referenced and fascinating philosophical conundrums are posed. The book *What We Owe to Each Other* (1998) by American philosopher T. M. Scanlon (b. 1940) is a key motif.

One of the questions frequently posed in the series is whether the study of philosophy can make one a better person. To this, *The Good Place* offers a resounding Yes. All of the main characters in the series develop as persons and become more thoughtful and less selfish as they ponder the great questions of philosophy. In a period of doubt and anxiety, this note of optimism was welcome to many.

A c. 1896 German American lithograph titled *The Roads to Heaven and Hell*; although *The Good Place*'s "Good" and "Bad" places were not envisioned as religious conceptions of heaven and hell as shown here, having a morally developed outlook on life enabled each of the protagonists to eventually arrive at the Good Place.

SEE ALSO *The Consolation of Philosophy* (524)

Eurus
Ignis
Coler c°

Sophiam me Greci vocant Latini Sapienciam
Egipcii & Chaldei me inuenere Greci scripsere
Latini transtulere Germani ampliauer e :-

Zephir⁹
Aer
Sanguine⁹

EGIPCIORVM SACERDOTES ET CHALDEI

Pro   lont

PHILO   SOPHIA

SAPIENTES GERMANORVM

Albe   rtus

GRECORVM PHILOSOPHI

Pla   to

Θ
H
ΛΟ
ΓΗ
ΑΡ
ΡΘ
ΛΟ
ΓΕΛ
Φ

LATINORVM POETAE ET RHETORES

Cicero   Virgilius°

Boreas
Terra
Melancolic⁹

Quicquid habet Coelum quid Terra quid Aer & aequor
Quicquid in humanis Rebus & esse potest
Et deus in toto quicquid facit igneus orbe
Philosophia meo pectore cuncta gero :-

Auster
Aqua
Flecmatic⁹

Acknowledgments

I AM GRATEFUL TO ALL THE PROFESSORS who have taught me the history of philosophy, most especially Ken Merrill, Tom Boyd, J. N. Mohanty, Stewart Umphrey, R. T. Wallis, Paul Brown, Stephen Wykstra, John Robinson, Phil Quinn, Alfred Freddoso, and Neil Delaney. My colleagues Bernard Prusak and Bill Irwin have provided helpful feedback on their areas of expertise. I am grateful to them, and to my wife, Mia, without whose love and support this book could not have been written.

At Sterling Publishing, for their courtesy and skill, I am most grateful to project editor Barbara Berger, designer Christine Heun, photo editor Linda Liang, production editor Michael Cea, and cover designer and director Elizabeth Mihaltse Lindy.

OPPOSITE: Woodcut of "Philosophia" signed with the monogram of Albrecht Dürer. From *Qvatvor libri amorvm secvndvm qvatvor latera Germanie feliciter incipivnt*, 1502, by Conrad Celtes.

Further Reading and Sources

General Reading

Audi, Robert, ed. *The Cambridge Dictionary of Philosophy*. New York: Cambridge Univ. Press, 1995.

Copleston, Frederick. *A History of Philosophy*. 9 vols. New York: Image, 1946–75.

Durant, Will. *The Story of Philosophy*. New York: Pocket Books, 1991. Originally published in 1926.

Edwards, Paul, ed. *Encyclopedia of Philosophy*. 8 vols. New York: Macmillan, 1967.

Internet Encyclopedia of Philosophy, www.iep.utm. edu. Kenny, Anthony. *A New History of Western Philosophy*. Oxford, UK: Clarendon Press, 2010.

Lavine, T. Z. *From Socrates to Sartre*. New York: Bantam, 1985.

Magee, Bryan. *The Story of Philosophy*. London: DK, 1998.

Parkinson, G. H. R., and Stuart Shanker, eds. *Routledge History of Philosophy*. 10 vols. New York: Routledge, 1993–2003.

Russell, Bertrand. *A History of Western Philosophy*. New York: Simon & Schuster, 1945.

Soccio, Douglas J. *Archetypes of Wisdom: An Introduction to Philosophy*. 9th ed. Belmont, CA: Wadsworth, 2015. *Stanford Encyclopedia of Philosophy*, plato.stanford.edu.

Sources

c. 585 BCE / Birth of Western Philosophy: Guthrie, W. K. C. *A History of Greek Philosophy*. Vol. 1, *The Earlier Presocratics and the Pythagoreans*. Cambridge, UK: Cambridge Univ. Press, 1962.

c. 550 BCE / The Dao: Chan, Alan. "Laoxi." *Stanford Encyclopedia of Philosophy*, http://plato.stanford. edu/ entries/laozi/.

c. 540 BCE / Reincarnation: Barnes, Jonathan. *The Presocratic Philosophers*, rev. ed. London: Routledge & Kegan Paul, 1983.

c. 540 BCE / Ahimsa: Webb, Mark Owen. "Jain Philosophy." *Internet Encyclopedia of Philosophy*, http://www.iep.utm.edu/jain/.

c. 525 BCE / The Four Noble Truths: Hanh, Thich Nhat. *The Heart of the Buddha's Teaching*. New York: Broadway Books, 1999.

c. 525 BCE / No-Self (Anatta): Siderits, Mark. "Buddha." *Stanford Encyclopedia of Philosophy*, http://plato. stanford.edu/entries/buddha/.

c. 500 BCE / Confucian Ethics: Huang, Chichung, trans. *The Analects of Confucius*. Oxford, UK: Oxford Univ. Press, 1997.

c. 500 BCE /Reciprocity: Yutang, Lin, ed. and trans. *The Wisdom of Confucius*. New York: Modern Library, 1938.

c. 500 BCE / Change Is Constant: Graham, Daniel. "Heraclitus." *Stanford Encyclopedia of Philosophy*, http://plato. stanford.edu/entries/heraclitus/.

c. 450 BCE / Protagoras and Relativism: Poster, Carol. "Protagoras." *Internet Encyclopedia of Philosophy*, http://www.iep. utm.edu/protagor/.

c. 450 BCE / The Sophists: Kerferd, G. B. *The Sophistic Movement*. Cambridge, UK: Cambridge Univ. Press, 1981.

c. 450 BCE / Ladder of Love: Waithe, Mary Ellen, ed. *A History of Women Philosophers*. Dordrecht, Netherlands: Klewer, 1987.

c. 430 BCE / Know Thyself: Guthrie, W. K. C. *Socrates*. Cambridge, UK: Cambridge Univ. Press, 1969.

c. 420 BCE / Atoms and the Void: Bailey, Cyril. *The Greek Atomists and Epicurus*. New York: Russell and Russell, 1964.

c. 420 BCE / Universal Love: Loy, Hu-chieh. "Mozi." *Internet Encyclopedia of Philosophy*, http://www.iep. utm.edu/mozi/.

c. 400 BCE / Cynicism: Guthrie, W. K. C. *The Sophists*. Cambridge, UK: Cambridge Univ. Press, 1969.

c. 400 BCE / Cyrenaic Hedonism: O'Keefe, Tim / "Aristippus." *Internet Encyclopedia of Philosophy*, http://www. iep.utm.edu/aristip/.

c. 400 BCE / The Bhagavad Gita: Radhakrishnan, Sarvepalli. *The Bhagavadgita*. New York: Harper & Row, 1973.

399 BCE / The Trial and Death of Socrates: Stone, I. F. *The Trial of Socrates*. New York: Doubleday, 1988.

c. 399 BCE / Socratic Dialogues: Vlastos, Gregory. *Socrates: Ironist and Moral Philosopher*. Ithaca, NY: Cornell Univ. Press, 1991.

c. 380 BCE / Mind-Body Dualism: Grube, G. M. A. *Plato's Thought.* 2nd ed. Indianapolis, IN: Hackett, 1980.

c. 380 BCE / Plato's Republic: Annas, Julia. *An Introduction to Plato's Republic.* New York: Oxford Univ. Press, 1981.

c. 367 BCE / Aristotle Enrolls in the Academy: Guthrie, W. K. C. *A History of Greek Philosophy.* Vol. 6, *Aristotle: An Encounter.* Cambridge, UK: Cambridge Univ. Press, 1981.

c. 330 BCE / Nicomachean Ethics: Urmson, J. O. *Aristotle's Ethics.* Oxford, UK: Blackwell, 1988.

c. 320 BCE / Maybe Life Is a Dream: Hansen, Chad. "Zhuangzi." *Stanford Encyclopedia of Philosophy,* http://plato. stanford.edu/entries/zhuangzi/.

c. 300 BCE / Epicureanism: Rist, John M. *Epicurus: An Introduction.* Cambridge, UK: Cambridge Univ. Press, 1972.

c. 300 BCE / Stoicism: Sandbach, F. H. *The Stoics.* 2nd ed. Indianapolis, IN: Hackett, 1994.

c. 300 BCE / Innate Goodness: Yu-Lan, Fung. *A History of Chinese Philosophy.* Translated by Derk Bodde. Princeton, NJ: Princeton Univ. Press, 1953.

51 BCE / Universal Moral Law: Nicgorski, Walter, ed. *Cicero's Practical Philosophy.* Notre Dame, IN: Univ. of Notre Dame Press, 2012.

c. 125 / Epictetian Stoicism: Rist, J. M. *Stoic Philosophy.* Cambridge, UK: Cambridge Univ. Press, 1969.

180 / The Philosopher-King: Hadot, Pierre. *The Inner Citadel: The Meditations of Marcus Aurelius.* Translated by Michael Chase. Cambridge, MA: Harvard Univ. Press, 1998.

c. 200 / Outlines of Pyrrhonism: Annas, Julia, and Jonathan Barnes. *The Modes of Skepticism.* Cambridge, UK: Cambridge Univ. Press, 1985.

c. 250 / Neoplatonism: O'Meara, Dominic J. *Plotinus: An Introduction to the Enneads.* Oxford, UK: Clarendon Press, 1993.

386 / Augustine's Conversion: Brown, Peter. *Augustine of Hippo: A Biography.* Berkeley: Univ. of California Press, 2000.

c. 520 / Origins of Chan/Zen Buddhism: Watts, Alan. *The Way of Zen.* New York: Pantheon, 1957.

524 / The Consolation of Philosophy: Marenbon, John. *Boethius.* Oxford, UK: Oxford Univ. Press, 2003.

c. 810 / Monism: Radhakrishnan, Sarvepalli. *Indian Philosophy.* Vol. 1. London: George Allen & Unwin, 1923.

1078 / The Ontological Argument: Davies, Brian, and Brian Leftow, eds. *The Cambridge Companion to Anselm.* New York: Cambridge Univ. Press, 2005.

c. 1265 / The Great Medieval Synthesis: Davies, Brian. *The Thought of Thomas Aquinas.* Oxford, UK: Oxford Univ. Press, 1993; Stump, Eleonore. *Aquinas.* New York: Routledge, 2005.

c. 1265 / The Five Ways: Kenny, Anthony. *The Five Ways.* New York: Routledge, 2008.

c. 1270 / Natural Law: Murphy, Mark. "The Natural Law Tradition in Ethics." *Stanford Encyclopedia of Philosophy,* http://plato.stanford.edu/entries/ natural-law-ethics/.

c. 1320 / Ockham's Razor: Spade, Paul Vincent. "William of Ockham." *Stanford Encyclopedia of Philosophy,* http:// plato.stanford.edu/entries/ ockham/.

c. 1350 / The Renaissance Begins: Durant, Will. *The Renaissance.* New York: Simon & Schuster, 1953.

1516 / Utopia: Baker-Smith, Dominic. *More's Utopia.* Toronto: Univ. of Toronto Press, 2000.

c. 1520 / The Humanist Ideal: Nauert, Charles. "Desiderius Erasmus." *Stanford Encyclopedia of Philosophy,* http://plato.stanford.edu/entries/ erasmus/.

1532 / The Prince: Pocock, J. G. A. *The Machiavellian Moment: Florentine Political Thought and the Atlantic Republican Tradition.* Princeton, NJ: Princeton Univ. Press, 1975.

1543 / The Birth of Modern Science: Butterfield, Herbert. *The Origins of Modern Science.* Rev. ed. New York: Free Press, 1997.

1620 / The Enlightenment Begins: Durant, Will, and Ariel Durant. *The Age of Reason Begins.* New York: Simon & Schuster, 1961.

1637 / The Father of Modern Philosophy: Kenny, Anthony. *Descartes: A Study of His Philosophy.* New York: Random House, 1968.

1641 / Meditations on First Philosophy: Cottingham, John, ed. *The Cambridge Companion to Descartes.* New York: Cambridge Univ. Press, 1992.

1651 / Leviathan: Sorell, Tom, ed. *The Cambridge Companion to Hobbes.* Cambridge, UK: Cambridge Univ. Press, 1996.

1651 / Free Will and Determinism Are Compatible: McKenna, Michael, and D. Justin Coates. "Compatibilism." *Stanford Encyclopedia of Philosophy*, http://plato.stanford.edu/entries/compatibilism/.

1670 / Pascal's Wager: Morris, Thomas V. *Making Sense of It All: Pascal and the Meaning of Life.* Grand Rapids, MI: Wm. B. Eerdmans, 1992.

1677 / Ethics: Bennett, Jonathan. *A Study of Spinoza's Ethics.* Indianapolis, IN: Hackett, 1984.

1689 / Human Rights: Simmons, A. John. *The Lockean Theory of Rights.* Princeton, NJ: Princeton Univ. Press, 1992.

1689 / Religious Liberty: Tuckness, Alex. "Locke's Political Philosophy." *Stanford Encyclopedia of Philosophy*, http://plato.stanford.edu/entries/locke-political/.

1689 / Empiricism: Ayers, Michael. *Locke: Epistemology and Ontology.* London: Routledge, 1991.

1713 / To Be Is to Be Perceived: Pitcher, George. *Berkeley.* London: Routledge, 1999. First published 1977 by Routledge & Kegan Paul.

1725 / The Moral Sense: Kauppinen, Antti. "Moral Sentimentalism." *Stanford Encyclopedia of Philosophy*, http://plato.stanford.edu/entries/moral-sentimentalism/.

1730 / Deism: Stephen, Leslie. *History of English Thought in the Eighteenth Century.* 2 vols. 1876. Reprint, London: Forgotten Books, 2012.

1739 / A Treatise of Human Nature: Stroud, Barry. *Hume.* New York: Routledge & Kegan Paul, 1977.

1739 / The Problem of Induction: Salmon, Wesley C. *The Foundations of Scientific Inference.* Pittsburgh, PA: Univ. of Pittsburgh Press, 1967.

1748 / An Attack on Miracles: Norton, David Fate, and Jacqueline Taylor, eds. *The Cambridge Companion to Hume.* New York: Cambridge Univ. Press, 1993.

1751 / Morality Is Rooted in Feeling: Norton, David Fate. *David Hume: Common-Sense Moralist, Skeptical Metaphysician.* Princeton, NJ: Princeton University Press, 1982.

1759 / Candide: Durant, Will, and Ariel Durant. *The Age of Voltaire.* New York: Simon & Schuster, 1965.

c. 1760 / The Birth of Romanticism: Berlin, Isaiah. *The Roots of Romanticism.* Princeton, NJ: Princeton Univ. Press, 1999.

1762 / The Social Contract: Bertram, Christopher. *Rousseau and The Social Contract.* London: Routledge, 2004.

1762 / Emile and Natural Education: Rorty, Amélie Oksenberg, ed. *Philosophers on Education.* New York: Routledge, 1998.

1770 / A Godless, Mechanistic Universe: Copleston, Frederick. *A History of Philosophy. Vol. 6, Modern Philosophy: The French Enlightenment to Kant.* Westminster, MD: Newman Press, 1960.

1779 / Hume's Dialogues: Gaskin, J. C. A. *Hume's Philosophy of Religion.* London: Macmillan, 1987.

1781 / Critique of Pure Reason: Guyer, Paul, ed. *The Cambridge Companion to Kant.* New York: Cambridge Univ. Press, 1992.

1785 / The Categorical Imperative: Aune, Bruce. *Kant's Theory of Morals.* Princeton, NJ: Princeton Univ. Press, 1979.

1787 / The Federalist: Wills, Garry. *Explaining America: The Federalist.* New York: Doubleday, 1981.

1789 / Utilitarianism: Harrison, Ross. *Bentham.* London: Routledge, 1999.

1792 / A Vindication of the Rights of Woman: Tomaselli, Sylvana. "Mary Wollstonecraft." *Stanford Encyclopedia of Philosophy*, http:// plato.stanford.edu/entries/wollstonecraft/.

1819 / The Philosophy of Pessimism: Magee, Bryan. *The Philosophy of Schopenhauer.* Rev. ed. Oxford, UK: Clarendon Press, 1997.

1836 / American Transcendentalism: Gura, Philip F. *American Transcendentalism: A History.* New York: Hill & Wang, 2008.

1843 / Existentialism: Hannay, Alistair. *Kierkegaard.* New York: Routledge, 1999.

1846 / Truth Is Subjectivity: Barrett, William. *Irrational Man: A Study in Existential Philosophy.* Garden City, NY: Doubleday, 1962.

1854 / Walden: Richardson, Robert D., Jr. *Henry Thoreau: A Life of the Mind.* Berkeley: Univ. of California Press, 1986.

1859 / On Liberty: Ten, C. L. *Mill's On Liberty.* Oxford, UK: Clarendon Press, 1980.

1862 / Social Darwinism: Hofstadter, Richard. *Social Darwinism in American Thought.* Boston: Beacon Press, 1990.

1863 / Refined Utilitarianism: Skorupski, John, ed. *The Cambridge Companion to John Stuart Mill.* Cambridge, UK: Cambridge Univ. Press, 1998.

1878 / Origins of Pragmatism: Hookway, Christopher. *Peirce*. London: Routledge, 1985.

1882 / "God Is Dead": Kaufmann, Walter. *Nietzsche: Philosopher, Psychologist, Antichrist*. 3rd ed. New York: Random House, 1968.

1882 / Perspectivism: Hollingdale, R. J. *Nietzsche: The Man and His Philosophy*. Rev. ed. Cambridge, UK: Cambridge Univ. Press, 1999.

1887 / The Revaluation of Values: Leiter, Brian. "Nietzsche's Moral and Political Philosophy." *Stanford Encyclopedia of Philosophy*, http://plato.stanford.edu/entries/nietzsche-moral-political/.

1897 / "The Will to Believe": Gale, Richard M. *The Philosophy of William James: An Introduction*. Cambridge, UK: Cambridge Univ. Press, 2005.

1900 / Phenomenology: Smith, Barry, and David Woodruff Smith, eds. *The Cambridge Companion to Husserl*. Cambridge, UK: Cambridge Univ. Press, 1995.

1903 / Ethical Intuitionism: Baldwin, Tom. "George Edward Moore." *Stanford Encyclopedia of Philosophy*, http://plato.stanford.edu/entries/moore/.

1907 / Pragmatism: Flower, Elizabeth, and Murray G. Murphey. *A History of American Philosophy*. Vol. 2. Indianapolis, IN: Hackett, 1977.

1916 / Progressive Education: Dykhuizen, George. *The Life and Mind of John Dewey*. Carbondale: Southern Illinois Univ. Press, 1973.

1923 / I and Thou: Schilpp, Paul Arthur, and Maurice S. Friedman, eds. *The Philosophy of Martin Buber*. LaSalle, IL: Open Court, 1967.

1925 / Instrumentalism: Tiles, J. E. *Dewey*. London: Routledge, 1988.

1927 / Being and Time: Dreyfus, H. L. *Being-in-the World: A Commentary of Heidegger's* Being and Time. Cambridge, MA: MIT Press, 1991.

1927 / Religion as Wish Fulfillment: Küng, Hans. *Freud and the Problem of God*. Rev. ed. Translated by Edward Quinn. New Haven, CT: Yale Univ. Press, 1990.

1930 / Deontological Intuitionism: Feldman, Fred. *Introductory Ethics*. Englewood Cliffs, NJ: Prentice Hall, 1978.

1936 / Logical Positivism: Foster, John. *Ayer*. London: Routledge, 2009.

1938 / Nausea: Lavine, T. Z. *From Socrates to Sartre: The Philosophic Quest*. New York: Bantam, 1985.

1942 / Existential Defiance: Aronson, Ronald. "Albert Camus." *Stanford Encyclopedia of Philosophy*, http://plato.stanford.edu/entries/camus/.

1946 / Atheistic Existentialism: Howells, Christina, ed. *The Cambridge Companion to Sartre*. Cambridge, UK: Cambridge Univ. Press, 1992.

1949 / The Second Sex: Mussett, Shannon. "Simone de Beauvoir." *Internet Encyclopedia of Philosophy*, http://www.iep.utm.edu/beauvoir/.

1949 / Ecocentrism: DesJardins, Joseph R. *Environmental Ethics*. 5th ed. Boston: Wadsworth, 2013.

1953 / Philosophical Investigations: Grayling, A. C. *Wittgenstein: A Very Short Introduction*. Oxford, UK: Oxford Univ. Press, 2001.

1962 / Scientific Revolutions: Nickles, Thomas, ed. *Thomas Kuhn*. Cambridge, UK: Univ. of Cambridge Press, 2003.

1966 / Soul-Making Theodicy: Tooley, Michael. "The Problem of Evil." *Stanford Encyclopedia of Philosophy*, http://plato.stanford.edu/entries/evil/.

1967 / Deconstruction: Norris, Christopher. *Derrida*. London: Routledge, 1987.

1971 / A Theory of Justice: Daniels, Norman, ed. *Reading Rawls*. Stanford, CA: Stanford Univ. Press, 1989.

1974 / Political Libertarianism: Paul, Jeffrey, ed. *Reading Nozick*. Totowa, NJ: Rowman & Littlefield, 1981.

1974 / "What Is It Like to Be a Bat?": Kim, Jaegwon. *Philosophy of Mind*. 3rd ed. Boulder, CO: Westview Press, 2011.

1975 / Animal Liberation: Sunstein, Cass R., and Martha C. Nussbaum, eds. *Animal Rights: Current Debates and New Directions*. New York: Oxford Univ. Press, 2004.

1975 / Power/Knowledge: Gutting, Gary, ed. *The Cambridge Companion to Foucault*. 2nd ed. New York: Cambridge Univ. Press, 2005.

c. 1976 / Emergence of Feminist Philosophy: Stone, Alison. *An Introduction to Feminist Philosophy*. Cambridge, UK: Polity Press, 2007.

1977 / Moral Anti-Realism: Joyce, Richard. "Moral Anti-Realism." *Stanford Encyclopedia of Philosophy*, http://plato.stanford.edu/entries/moral-anti-realism/.

1979 / Postmodernism: Woodward, Ashley. "Jean-François Lyotard." *Internet Encyclopedia of Philosophy*, http://www.iep.utm.edu/lyotard/.

1980 / The Chinese Room: Cole, David. "The Chinese Room Argument." *Stanford Encyclopedia of Philosophy*, http://plato.stanford.edu/entries/chinese-room/.

1981 / The Revival of Virtue Ethics: Hursthouse, Rosalind. *On Virtue Ethics*. Oxford, UK: Oxford Univ. Press, 1999.

1982 / In a Different Voice: Sander-Staudt, Maureen. "Care Ethics." *Internet Encyclopedia of Philosophy*, http://www.iep.utm.edu/care-eth/.

1984 / Revival of Christian Philosophy: Sennett, James F., ed. *The Analytic Theist: An Alvin Plantinga Reader*. Grand Rapids, MI: Eerdmans, 1998.

1989 / Religious Pluralism: Quinn, Philip L., and Kevin Meeker, eds. *The Challenge of Religious Diversity*. New York: Oxford Univ. Press, 1999.

1991 / Philosophical Zombies: Searle, John R. *The Mystery of Consciousness*. New York: New York Review of Books, 1997.

2000 / The Capability Approach: Robeyns, Ingrid. "The Capability Approach." *Stanford Encyclopedia of Philosophy*, http://plato.stanford.edu/entries/capability-approach/.

2004 / The New Atheists: Haught, John F. *God and the New Atheism*. Louisville, KY: Westminster John Knox Press, 2008.

2006 / Cosmopolitanism: Kleingeld, Pauline, and Eric Brown. "Cosmopolitanism." *Stanford Encyclopedia of Philosophy*, http://plato.stanford.edu/entries/cosmopolitanism/.

2016 / The Good Place: Engels, Kimberly S., and William Erwin, eds. *The Good Place and Philosophy: Everything is Forking Fine!* Hoboken, NJ: Wiley-Blackwell, 2021.

Picture Credits

Alamy: Album: 207; ARCHIVO GBB: 152; ©Bassco CANNARSA/Agence Opale: 250; ©Nancy Kaszerman/ZUMA Press: 249; Pictorial Press Ltd.: 181; Sueddeutsche Zeitung Photo: 233; Neil Turner: 238

Depositphotos.com: ©Georgios: 144; ©Mliss: 241; ©Nicku: 135; ©SimpleFoto: 225

Europeana: 69; courtesy of The Royal Library: The National Library of Denmark and Copenhagen University Library: 160

Getty Images: Bettmann: 226; DigitalVision Vectors: duncan1890: 74; Grafissimo: 40, 222; traveler1116: 219; ZU_09: 126; E+: traveler1116: 219; iStock/Getty Images Plus: denisk0: 113; ivan-96: 149; wynnter: 64, 157

Courtesy of Harvard Art Museums: Belinda L. Randall from the collection of John Witt Randall: 22

Internet Archive: 17

Courtesy of The J. Paul Getty Museum, Los Angeles: 12

Library of Congress: 172, 198, 253

Courtesy of The Metropolitan Museum of Art, New York: 25

National Gallery of Art: 26

Rijksmuseum: 5, 11, 29, 48, 79, 81, 93, 102, 110, 118

Shutterstock.com: Charlesimage: 32; Ezhevika: I; ViRtuA: 38

Wellcome Collection: 8, 37, 45, 99, 128

Courtesy of Wikimedia Commons: 53, 59, 105, 125, 128, 143, 163, 164; Arquivo Nacional Collection: 191; Brazilian National Archive: 201; Joop Bilsen/Anefo/Nationaal Archief: 188; Robin Holland: 246; Houghton Library, Harvard University, Typ 520.02.269: 254

Courtesy of Yale University: Beinecke Rare Book and Manuscript Library: 90

Index

Page numbers in *italics* include illustrations and photographs

Holbach, Baron d' (Paul-Henri Thiry), 140–41
Humanist ideal, 92–93
Human rights, 98, 112–13
Hume, David
  attack on miracles, 128–29
  Dialogues of, 142–43
  empiricism and, 119, 124–125, 128–29
  engraving of, *126*
  Holbach and, 141
  Kant and, 145
  morality rooted in feeling, 130–31
  problem of induction, 126–27
  A Treatise of Human Nature, 124–25
Husserl, Edmund, 180–81
Hutcheson, Francis, 120–21, 130–31

I and Thou (Buber), 188–89
Idealism, 119
In a Different Voice (Gilligan), 238–39
Induction, problem of, 126–27
Instrumentalism, 190–91
Intuitionism, deontological, 196–97
Intuitionism, ethical, 182–83
Irwin, William, 252

Jaggar, Alison, 228
Jainism, 10–11
James, William, 178–79, 184–85
Jay, John, 148
Jesus of Nazareth (Jesus Christ)
  engraving of, *171*
  Golden Rule and, 18, 146
  mural of, 241
  preaching of, 33
Jnana yoga, 39
John XXII (pope), 86
Justice, liberal theory of, 218–19
Kalpa Sutra, *11*
Kant, Immanuel
  birth of Romanticism and, 134

categorical imperative, 146–47
ethical decision procedure and, 236
moral judgments and, 204
Critique of Pure Reason, 144–45
engraving of, *144*
Schopenhauer and, 155
Karma yoga, 39
Kierkegaard, Søren, 158–59, *160–61*
"Know thyself" (Socrates), 28–29
Krishna, *38–39*
Kuhn, Thomas, 212–13

Ladder of love, 26–27
Language, 210, 211, 217, 227, 233, 234
Laozi, 6–7
Law
  civil liberty and, 137, 165
  natural, 60–61, 84–85, 112
  universal moral, 60–61
Leopold, Aldo, 208–9
Leucippus, 30–31
Leviathan (Hobbes), 104–5
Libertarianism, political, 220–21
Liberty, Mill's book on, 164–65
Liberty, religious, 114–15
Locke, John, 96, 112–13, 114–15, 116–17, 119
Logical positivism, 198–99
Logos, 20–21
Love
  ladder of, 26–27
  universal, 32–33
Luther, Martin, 92, 93
Lyotard, Jean-François, 232–33

Machiavelli, Niccolò, 94–95
MacIntyre, Alasdair, 237
Mackie, John Leslie, 230–31
Madison, James, 148–49
Mahavira, 10–11
Marcus Aurelius, *64*–65
Mechanistic, godless universe, 140–41
Medieval synthesis, 80–81

Meditations on First Philosophy (Descartes), 102–3
Mencius (Mengzi), 58–*59*
Metaphysics, 79, 145, 199
Mill, John Stuart, 153, *164*–65, 168–69, 236
Mind-body dualism, 44–45
Miracles, attack on, 128–29
Modern philosophy, father of. *See* Descartes, René
Monism, 76–77
Moore, George Edward, 182–83
Morality. *See also* ethics
  categorical imperative and, 146–47
  deontological intuitionism and, 196–97
  Golden Rule and, 18–19, 146
  moral anti-realism, 230–31
  moral sense, 120–21
  natural law and, 84–85
  reciprocity and, 18–19
  refined utilitarianism and, 172–73
  revaluation of values, 176–77
  rooted in feeling, 130–31
  universal moral law, 60–61
More, Sir Thomas, 90–91
Mozi (Mo-tzu), *32*–33
Muir, John, 134, 162

Naess, Arne, 208
Nagel, Thomas, 222–23
Natural law, 60–61, 84–85, 86, 112
Nausea (Sartre), 200–201
Neoplatonism, 68–69
New Atheists, 248–49
Newcomen, Thomas, *143*
Nicomachean Ethics (Aristotle), 50–51
Nietzsche, Friedrich
  drawing of, *172*
  "God Is Dead," 172–73
  perspectivism, 174–75
  revaluation of values, 176–77
No-self (*anatta*), 14–15
Novum Organum (Francis Bacon), 99